T0195931

Zen Centered : Healing Your Intuitive Body

Master the Art of Radical Self Care

SAGE PHOENIX

BALBOA.PRESS
A DIVISION OF HAY HOUSE

Copyright © 2020 Sage Phoenix.

All rights reserved. No part of this book may be used or reproduced by any means, graphic, electronic, or mechanical, including photocopying, recording, taping or by any information storage retrieval system without the written permission of the author except in the case of brief quotations embodied in critical articles and reviews.

The information, ideas, and suggestions in this book are not intended as a substitute for professional medical advice. Before following any suggestions contained in this book, you should consult your personal physician. Neither the author nor the publisher shall be liable or responsible for any loss or damage allegedly arising as a consequence of your use or application of any information or suggestions in this book.

Balboa Press books may be ordered through booksellers or by contacting:

Balboa Press
A Division of Hay House
1663 Liberty Drive
Bloomington, IN 47403
www.balboapress.com
1 (877) 407-4847

Because of the dynamic nature of the Internet, any web addresses or links contained in this book may have changed since publication and may no longer be valid. The views expressed in this work are solely those of the author and do not necessarily reflect the views of the publisher, and the publisher hereby disclaims any responsibility for them.

The author of this book does not dispense medical advice or prescribe the use of any technique as a form of treatment for physical, emotional, or medical problems without the advice of a physician, either directly or indirectly. The intent of the author is only to offer information of a general nature to help you in your quest for emotional and spiritual well-being. In the event you use any of the information in this book for yourself, which is your constitutional right, the author and the publisher assume no responsibility for your actions.

Any people depicted in stock imagery provided by Getty Images are models, and such images are being used for illustrative purposes only. Certain stock imagery © Getty Images.

Print information available on the last page.

ISBN: 978-1-9822-4125-4 (sc)
ISBN: 978-1-9822-4126-1 (e)

Balboa Press rev. date: 01/31/2020

CONTENTS

INTRODUCTION :

<u>Zen Centered</u> is a testimonial to what I've learned from my life's work as a holistic healer and my own personal healing journey. They are one in the same. After over twenty five years of helping women heal from traumatic grief, depression, eating disorders and other psychosomatic distress, I write this Radical Self Care guide to share with you what I've learned about healing our Intuitive Bodies. We can learn how to heal the mysterious psychosomatic symptoms that cause us suffer and reverse the cycle of burn out. this guide will help you learn how.

<u>Zen Centered Holistic Healing Principles and Practices for Radical Self Care of the Intuitive Body</u>

1. Whole Person Healing : Body Mind and Spirit
2. Holistic Lifestyle Remedies to Restore and Renew the Intuitive Body
   a. Whole Foods as Medicines
   b. Plants as Natural Medicines
   c. Yoga as Medicine : Music Sound Movement
3. Mindfulness as Medicine for the Mind to Heal the Body

<u>Personal Narrative</u> : You know how it is…you pride your self in being healthy, fit and active in your life, busy building your new business dream. Then the unexpected happens – a big ford truck rear ends your little hybrid car and you end up with a bad case of whiplash. Just when you recover your self enough to get back on your feet, your landlord dies and his heir wants to remodel your property.

When you're moving out of the house you called home, A box drops on your foot and a hairline fracture takes you down and out for another six months of your mid-life. "no big deal," you tell your self, "I'll be back on my feet in no time." Haha. Sounds good but then reality sets in.

In the real world, "No time at all" stretches into weeks and then months, I find myself restless, angry and despairing. I can barely move but my mind is running away with my optimism. as my mind becomes my own worst enemy, my thoughts become dark and pessimistic, lost in the shadows. this is my story of how I recovered my self from an epic fall that turned into a mental health crisis I was embarrassed to have.

Radical Self Care was the miracle I was called upon to create in my own life – once I faced my own descent into depressing thoughts and despairing feelings. My call to awaken. This healing journey is what has inspired me to record the lessons I have learned and share them with you in Zen Centered: Healing Your Intuitive Body.

If you are ready to let go of distracting your self into a medical or mental health crisis, Zen Centered is here to help you to navigate your way through the darkness into insight and understanding.

Disclosures and Disclaimers :

This book is not meant to act as psychological treatment or substitute for any psychological treatment you may be receiving for depression, anxiety or post traumatic stress.

This book IS meant to be a supportive resource to help improve the way you take care of your physical mental and emotional well being.

Although all practices in Zen Centered are safe restorative and not psychologically invasive, I cannot predict your response nor am I responsible or liable for any undesired outcome you may experience. Always listen to your own Body for the limits that support and allow you to heal at your own pace.

If you have a history of severe trauma, suicidal depression or other serious mental illness, consult with your treatment specialist about how you use the exercise in this book to support your therapeutic process. If you experience any trauma symptoms like suicidal feelings, flashbacks, nightmares or intrusive memories, immediately seek assistance from a skilled trauma specialist in your local community.

Do not practice any vigorous Yoga Flow sequences or inversions if you have been diagnosed with medical conditions like high blood pressure. If you are taking prescription medications for any medical condition, always consult with your prescribing physician before you begin any new physical exercise plan or vigorous vinyasa practice.

All yoga practices found in this guide are restorative or foundational poses that are designed to be practiced in slow and gentle movements. The poses or pose sequences are restorative based and supported by science to improve the rest and relaxation response of the body. They are safe and low risk when you practice as guided and take measures to ensure your body is supported.

Disclosure : any "personal narratives" or journal entries or references made to clients are either my own personal experience OR composite sketches of real people who do not exist. The narratives are real life stories but are not any one person's story. Any and all confidential material shared in my work with clients remains now and forever privileged information.

Chapter : Sobering Statistics : Our Collective Mental Health Crises :

- ~ The World Organization of Health estimates at least 300 million people worldwide are suffering from depression.
- ~ 20 million women in the united States suffer from an eating disorder at one point in her lifetime.
- ~ Over 40 million women in the United States is suffering from an anxiety disorder. Anxiety is one of the most common and pervasive mental health conditions in the U.S.

Despite advances in medicine, psychosomatic illnesses are on the rise!

What do your symptoms reveal about how you are struggling?

THE INTUITIVE BODY

"The Body is Precious…it is your vehicle for awakening" **Buddha**

Chapter : The Body creates symptoms for a Reason!

The Body is Precious…

Is this how you relate to your Body? Do you treat your Body with respect and reverence as if she is a source of awakening?

Do you pay attention to your Body's intuitive wisdom -- or do you tend to distract, deny and ignore your dis-stress until you are ready to collapse?

Are you running on empty but afraid to admit you are sick and tired and miserable?

You've come to the right place.

My wake up call can be yours too. If I could heal with the tools I write about in this book, you can too. We all have the capacity to trust our Bodies more than not. When we do trust our Intuitive Body, healing is not only possible, it is inevitable.

This book was especially designed to share with you simple holistic medicines you might not know about. I want you to know you have the power to heal your Body and begin to make simple changes now.

Because there is no time like the Present.

Begin the healing now

A Mental Health Crisis: Burn Out:

Another sobering reality : "Burn out" has become so prevalent, it was defined as a medical condition until it was reclassified as a work related condition.

Topic : Classic Burn out symptoms : how are depression and burn out similar body mind problems ? Consider the classic symptoms of major depressive episode :

- ~ depressed mood
- ~ chronic fatigue
- ~ loss of energy
- ~ loss of interest
- ~ loss of motivation

Personal Narrative : *My personal burn out profile showed up in ALL of the "fatalistic five" listed above. I could also relate to the word used for burn out -- "depersonalization" I often felt like I was having an out of body experience from the moment my eyes opened in the morning until I feel into a restless disturbed sleep. I occasionally flickered in and out of the awareness that my mind was not working very well and was rather preoccupied with themes of darkness and defeat. Denial serves us well – until it does not and the state of my overwhelming despair prompted me to take a pause myself.*

Topic 1 : What is the difference between depression and burnout?

According to Schonfeld IS, Bianchi R, Palazzi S at the Department of Psychology in The City College of the City University of New *York,*

Burnout is thought to be comprised of these key symptoms: *emotional exhaustion, depersonalization, and reduced personal accomplishment.*

Historically, however, burnout has been difficult to separate from depression because *the symptoms of burnout often coincide with symptoms of depression.* Just like burn out can be a response to either a series of emotional stressors or a major trauma disaster or tragedy that dramatically alters your life trajectory.

"Overall, burnout is likely to reflect a "classical" depressive process unfolding in reaction to unresolvable stress" https://www.ncbi.nlm.nih. gov/pubmed/30087493

Topic 2 : Stress As an Acceptable Form of Mental Illness : I took a pause when I read this – is this really acceptable to assume stress is either unresolvable or an acceptable "normal?" If burn out now has a medical category or condition, does it mean we need to now need to act as if it is like many other psychosomatic illnesses that remain a mystery and source of unnecessary suffering?

Mindful Inquiry : If our thoughts and beliefs effect how we feel physically, mentally and emotionally, what is the consequence of thinking stress is unresolvable? Science shows for every thought we have there is a positive or negative impact on our physical mental and emotional body. Does the idea that stress is unresolvable inspire a sense of hope – or may not so much.

<u>Persistent and Pervasive but Not Permanent</u> : Because the symptoms of *emotional exhaustion, depersonalization, and reduced personal accomplishment* were so persistent and pervasive amongst those who sought medical treatment, "burn out" was first classified as a medical condition until it was reclassified as a work place related stress.

Is it any wonder that despite the advances of modern day medicine, most doctors have reported an INCREASE in psychosomatic conditions?

According to some estimates, up to 90% of the illnesses doctors evaluate in their office are stress related and 80% of those medical conditions are preventable!

Eighty percent?

<u>Chapter : The Crisis We All Share :</u> In her book, Mind Over Medicine, Dr. Lissa Rankin says we are all experience close to 50 some stress reactions a day – which means our body is constantly activated to act in a fight flight or freeze state to cope with the dangers of every day life. There may not be lions roaring in our face or tigers threatening to eat us for breakfast, but our busy lifestyles filled with "goals" and

gadgets keep us in unconscious autopilot, hyper agitated and hyper vigilant unable to rest or relax.

Topic : Toxic Lifestyle Habits: Our "normal" state of day to day living can be a catalyst a cause or an aggravating source of emotional stress we deny! because in our culture to show our emotional vulnerability is often judged as weakness or a sign of a mental or moral defect, we often bury our emotional life and act as if we are not suffering when we are feeling "burnt out" "depressed" or "worried"

What I've learned from twenty five years and more as a holistic healer :

None of us is immune from suffering anxiety, depression or even post traumatic stress! we ALL need to heal the way we think about and approach our mental health and emotional concerns! We desperately need to break through the stigmas that keep us ashamed of our suffering.

"every life contains difficulties we are not prepared for." (Bernard Seigel, M.D.. Love Medicine & Miracles)

Breaking Through the Shame :

Do we have the same kind of shame if we suffer from diabetes or cancer or any other medical condition that needs to be healed?

I know we do not. In truth I believe part of our current medical health care crises reflects the dysfunction-ing relationship between our Intuitive Bodies and our shame about what we do not understand.

I believe When we approach our emotional illnesses without shame or bias in the way we do hypertension or diabetes or cancer, we will be healing our personal collective mental health crises. I am here to help you challenge the belief that we need to "accept" stress as an "acceptable" by sharing the tools I used to heal myself from the troubled state of my burnt out body mind and spirit.

Chapter : Challenge the Paradigm with Holistic Complementary Alternative Medicines

There is nothing acceptable about gushing blood from a gash in our leg – why should we accept depression as an acceptable way to say my heart is bleeding unspoken grief?

Is it really acceptable to accept chronic dis-ease or dis-stress as a way of life?

What else can we do but surrender to a medical system designed to categorize our symptoms and offer us prescription drugs or diagnostic tests to define our ill defined emotional distress?

Zen Centered is here to help you re-define what is acceptable so you can find better remedies than your current lifestyle habits. Heal the broken bond between your rational irrational mind and your Intuitive Body by tuning in to your Zen Center – your source of innate wisdom.

This is what else is possible:

- We can use holistic medicines – like mindfulness, movement and plants as remedies to reverse the cycle of burnt out, disconnected and depressed.
- We can turn to ancient traditions and healing medicines aligned with planet earth and the wisdom of Mother Nature.
- We can remember our Body knows how to heal. Do you Recall how your body has healed you from a wound a broken bone or an common illness?
- We can learn to re-think of our Symptoms as messages from the Intuitive body. Our pain can guide us into the healing we need to do for our physical, emotional and mental well being.
- We can choose wisely the antidotes we use to treat toxic burn out patterns and unhealthy habits we have unconsciously adapted.
- We can reverse the cycle of autopilot burn out by tuning in to the Intuitive Body.

Hello, this is a message from your Pain Body to your Intuitive Body.

Wake up, we need you

Paradigms and Patterns of Psychosomatic Illness :

STATISTICS : In a 2013 study done by the American Psychological Association American Institute cited :

1. 73% of Americans say they suffer from nervousness depression and irritability ;
2. 48% say they lose sleep over their worries;
3. 77% say they feel exhausted, tense or suffer from chronic headaches. Ugh!

Worse yet,

4. 48% overeat,
5. 39% skip eating altogether and
6. less than 33% can say they are active enough

My personal and professional experience with healing has taught me you do not need to accept the belief that stress is "unresolvable".

Nor do you need to deny or distract from your need to heal what hurts you. Awaken to the healing power of your Intuitive Body.

I know we do not need to accept the belief that "stress is unresolvable." when we are not unconsciously complicit in denying our pain, we can manage stress with simple holistic ways of healing.

Let Zen Centered be your guide to holistic ways you, too, can heal your Intuitive Body.

Shifting Paradigms of Pain with Zen Centered Radical Self Care

Miracle Cures, Miracle Drugs ? or the Miracle of the Intuitive Body:

- where do you place your trust?

Zen Centered Radical Self Care both reverses the cycle

of unhealthy Burn Out habits and heals the Intuitive Body's innate ability to restore rebalance and revitalize itself!

When you are ready to challenge Pain Body Beliefs like No Pain No Gain, you can reverse the cycle of feeling sick and tired and miserable pretending you are not!

Zen Centered will help you learn how to :

BECOME CONSCIOUS

- Where do you hurt? Instead of denying your pain and distracting with more busy-ness, you can become an ally in your own healing.

BECOME ACCOUNTABLE

- Treat your Intuitive Body with R-E-S-P-E-C-T
- AWAKEN to your Innate Ability to Heal

BECOME AWARE

- What Zen Centered Radical Self Care options appeal to your need to heal Burnt Out?
- What are your Pain Profiles and Pain Patterns that keep you dis-stressed and dis-eased?
- Practice – not per-fect – what you do to be more Present

BECOME INTENTIONAL

- ⁓ Choose from a Place of Awareness Insight and Intuitive Intelligence
- ⁓ How can you show your Body Reverence – or Respect- by the Radical Self Care plan you choose?

Overview of How to Do Radical Self Care. the details to be shared in future chapters

Radical self care is based on yoga principles and practices I've learned from ancient and modern yogi masters. I will quote them accordingly throughout the text and connect you with links to learn more from their teachings, including ancient masters like Patanjali, Hippocrates and Buddha as well as modern scientists and psychologists like Louise Hay, Carl Jung, Dr. Timothy McCall, Dr. Lissa Rankin as well as Dr. Gerberg.

I will also be sharing guided practices based on the healing principles I will be highlighting so you can begin to move into action now. In the present moment.

Topic : What You Need to Get Started :

1. A desire to become more conscious and aware of your own innate wisdom as a resource to heal restore and revitalize your body from your state of "burn out"
2. A commitment to change, learn and use the tools to transform you
3. A daily dedication to practice Radical self Care exercises to heal your Intuitive Body into your strength and optimal potential.
4. A willingness to take action in the Present to follow the Mindful Directives offered in this guide.
5. A readiness to let go of unhealthy habits that keep you from healing into your Intuitive Body wisdom and inherent strengths.

Reframe the Problem to Find a New Remedy as your Solution

FIRST THINGS FIRST: Redefine the problem!

Back to reframing the problem of Burn out.

Exercise : Mindful Journal : Do Inventory : Which of the pain points do you most relate to : of those you most relate to, rate the intensity of the symptom (1-10) and make note of the duration of the pain (a few minutes, a few hours, a few days, a few weeks, a few months)

- depressed mood
- chronic fatigue
- loss of energy
- loss of motivation
- loss of interest

Topic : What We Deny Does Not Disappear : One of my favorite doctors of psychology, Carl Jung teaches us about the dark side of the "shadow." just because we bury something, it does not disappear. In truth, the repressed emotional affect regresses into a more primitive form and causes MORE pain problems.

If it is true most of us use less than 10% of our brain's capacity for optimal functioning, isn't it time to wake up to what the other 90% of your brain could do for you?

If you say yes, to becoming more conscious, you are in the right place. Zen Centered is designed especially for you.

Topic : Toxic Relationships between the Body and the Mind : Pain Body vs. Intuitive Body

What if once you can admit the cause and the effect of what you think and how you feel, then you can become part of the solution – instead of stuck in the problem?

For example, let's go back to what we were just saying about ignoring or denying the impact of 50 some stress reactions in a day – what if you can reverse the cycle of burn out by actively engaging in Radical Self Care plans to reverse the negative impacts of unconscious stressors?

What if once you become more conscious, you can release the unconscious hold thought habits have on the way you are reacting to stress?

Wouldn't it be possible to make a new choice to do something else?

Of course it would be possible.

Chapter : Become Aware : Metaphysical Causations :

"You are your thoughts …everything you do rises from what you think…." Buddha

Topic 1 : In her book, <u>Heal your Body</u>, Louise Hay suggest we go beyond the physical to the mental cause to heal. She says, "An "incurable" disease cannot be cured by other means … We must go within to effect the cure. " For every positive or negative effect in our lives, there is a thought pattern that precedes it and maintains it. She encourages us to ask to reflect more deeply into what could be the thoughts that created this? Because Louise Hay understood that our consistent thought patterns create our experience – whether or not we are conscious of this influence.

what are the metaphysical causations behind your present state of dis-ease? ZC teaches you how to safely discover your Pain Belief Patterns so you can heal with the insights of your Intuitive Body.

BE CONSCIOUS

Topic One : <u>Know Thy Self!</u> Look to your own source of wisdom – your Intuitive Body. Tune in to discover how to heal the physical mental or emotional pain that is keeping you in a fight flight or freeze state of mind. Instead of doing your life on auto pilot, set your intentions to stop. Take a pause. Learn how to turn your attention inward with simple body mind awareness practices that shift your perspectives about what is possible.

<u>Topic Two</u> : <u>Uncover the mystery and the message</u> : What if you think of your psychosomatic symptoms as signals from your body of what you need to heal in your life?

<u>Chapter</u> : <u>The Relationship between Trauma and Burn Out</u> " it does not matter if it was the incessant terror of combat, trapped in a hurricane ..or an auto accident..all uncontrollable stress can have the *same biological impact.*"

In response to a life altering or life endangering event(s), Trauma *evokes a biological response* in the body. From <u>Waking the Tiger : Healing Trauma</u> :

"A maladaptive response is not necessarily a disease but a dis-ease – a discomfort that can range from mild uneasiness to panic or immobilization." (Peter Levine, <u>Waking the Tiger</u>)

This state of dis-ease can become debilitating unless the organism can respond in a fluid manner for the body and brain to process the experience. One of the problems for humans who go through trauma is our tendency to identify as survivors rather than *as animals with an instinctual power to heal.*

<u>Topic Two : Nature as a Model for Healing:</u> The animal's ability to rebound from threat can serve as a model for human healing. We need to pay better attention to our animal nature to find instinctive strategies needed to release us from trauma's debilitating effects. We need to learn to better listen to our Intuitive Body.

<u>The National Institute of Mental Health</u> studies show people who have gone through adverse life events – like unemployment, bereavement, psychological trauma, disasters or other tragic losses are MORE likely to develop depression.

Big T, Little t – the traumas we are exposed to on a day to day based is hard on the body mind and spirit! Modern day life can be hazardous to our mental, physical and emotional health and well being – until we become more conscious of our biologic response to overwhelming fear -- fight flight or freeze.

<u>Mindful Review</u> : Take a moment to consider how it FEELS to be running in autopilot:

1. do you feel like you are in a fight for your life?
2. do you feel like you are in flight, ready to take off before you even land?
3. do you feel frozen in a state of immobilized or stuck in a state of frustrated and frenzied?

<u>Chapter : Mindful Mind as an Awareness Tool and Practice</u>

<u>Topic 1 : Breaking through Barriers with Conscious Awareness</u>

Mindset blocks that keep us in burn out : denial, bargaining, justifying

Denial is a natural way of protecting our self against feeling helpless or ashamed ; yet this survivor response keeps us trapped in a state of fight-flight-freeze cycles of burn out.

Many of us inherently "know" there is something we need to confess or confide in to release us from the secret hell of burning out while pretending we are perfectly fine.

My experience has taught me – it is when we continue to deny our inherent sense of "knowingness," we only get more sick, tired and miserable than if we stop and tell the truth.

Because Dr. Jung was right all along when he said what we deny does not disappear, it falls into the shadow and becomes more even more primitive and aggressive in feeding our sense of despair and dis-ease.

<u>Topic 2: Becoming Mindful and Unconditionally Aware of the Power of A Mindful Mind</u>

Mindfulness is a pathway to insight and greater understanding of how the Body can be your ally in healing.

A Mindful Review allows you to observe to better understand the mysteries and messages your Intuitive Body sends you.

A Mindful Inquiry is NOT an inquisition where you are on trial. Learning how to become more Mindful in thought word and deed allows for an attitude of greater understanding and compassion. This kind of mindset allows for healing – and less harming.

Topic 3 : Cultivating Awareness through Radical Self Care Practices based in Holistic Medicine practices

Mindfulness challenges the idea that we need to be bullet proof and made of indestructible steel in defense of our feminine sensitivities.

Mindful Daily Practice is a way you stretch your Mind beyond the limitations of thought beliefs that over rule your divine Intuition.

Let us continue to see how we are ALL suffering more than is necessary to move forward into healing the isolation of feeling embarrassed and alienated in your secret nervous worries.

Mindful Inquiry : What about you?

If this is how you have been coping, what lies beneath? What are the sources and cites of potential for healing?

Chapter : The Power of Awareness : Breaking through Denial

Personal Narrative: *at first I couldn't accept my need to heal myself. I was too embarrassed to admit I was failing. Now I realize my only failure was in denying I was not woman made of steel. I was scared to admit I, too, was vulnerable.*

<u>Topic 1: Tune in to your Body's Messages</u> :

Do you listen to the message or is it a mystery why you are feeling so sick and tired …and sick and tired of it?

Topic 2 : <u>Your Body's Stress Response</u> can tell you if you are suffering from the cumulative build up of stress in a way that is unhealthy for your body.

Some doctors suggest we experience over 50 stress reactions a day and still others say we suffer from over 50,000 negative thoughts a day! 50,000?

Topic 3: <u>Every Thought is a Cause and has an Effect</u>

every thought you have has a physical, chemical response in the brain and the body. The brain releases mood chemicals – serotonin, norepinephrine, cortisol and adrenaline.

With every negative thought you think, your muscles become tight and tense; your heart beats faster, your hands begin to sweat and you may even feel dizzy.

<u>Chapter : Become Present to the Signals</u>

<u>YOUR BODY UNDER THE INFLUENCE OF STRESS:</u>

<u>Overactivated Sympathetic Nervous System</u> :

- ~ Cold hands or sweaty palms
- ~ Rapid heartbeat
- ~ Shortness in breath
- ~ Increase in blood pressure
- ~ Tight tense muscles

YOUR BODY UNDER THE INFLUENCE OF RELAXATION
RESPONSE :

Activated Parasympathetic Nervous System

- ~ Slow deep breathing
- ~ Slow and steady heart beat
- ~ Relaxed muscles
- ~ Palms cool and dry
- ~ Blood pressure stable

Chapter : The Science of the Brain and the Body : The Relationship Between Emotional Stress and Stressed Out

It is well known that prolonged emotional stress can lead to the chronic over-activation of the sympathetic nervous system (SNS) which doesn't bode well for the body. The life activating SNS is designed to interact in concert with the parasympathetic nervous system PNS and does so - unless impaired by highly demanding lifestyles and chronic emotional stressors.

The problem with chronic stress and highly demanding lifestyle habits? An over-activated Sympathetic Nervous System which creates symptoms like anxiety, agitation, insomnia, excess worry, hyper-reactivity, rapid and irregular heartbeats, elevated BP, GI distress, weight gain !

In our day to day conversation we might find ourselves saying things like "I'm burnt out," "I'm maxed out" "I'm so stressed out!" In most extreme cases, we can experience ALL of the symptoms of panic, PTSD and chronic fatigue on a recurring basis and become a catalyst for a medical emergency. This is because under high stress the body operates in a fight flight or freeze mode and is easily triggered into hyper reactive states.

The Parasympathetic Nervous System is as imperative to repairing and restoring body brain health as is the Sympathetic Nervous System to activating essential vital and executive functions of the brain and body.

When your Body and Brain are healthy and functioning at optimal capacity, there is a balance between rest and activity that supports vitality.

If, however, you have been operating under a highly demanding work home and family life schedule after suffering a highly emotional loss, tragedy or traumatic disaster event, you are more prone to developing psychosomatic symptoms. If you have grown up in a culture that dismisses pain as a sign of weakness and bravado as a way to manage adversity, you may find your self stymied by mysterious medical conditions because of your biases against emotional pain.

These human do do doing indestructible manifestos can unknowingly perpetuate our vulnerability towards anxiety, depression or psychosomatic ailments difficult to treat with most modern day medicines.

Chapter : The Problem of Burnt Out :

Pain Body Profiles and Patterns

As we dig deeper to uncover the consequences, the cause and the effects of living under the gun of overwhelming stress, we look to the Body's pain messages.

The biology of fight flight or freeze can express itself through what I call "pain body messages and pain body profiles"* because they share common patterns of pain we can target with Zen Centered Radical Self Care strategies.

*this concept of Pain Body is based on learnings from E. Tolle's work found in his book, The Power of Now. To learn more go here : www.thepowerofnow.com

Topic 1 : AGITATED DEPRESSION

Remember the Mindful Inquiries we made earlier about which of these Pain Body Profiles could you most relate to?

Which Pain Body Profile is most reflective of your Burn Out cycle?

This section offers you an opportunity to review the key pain points and pain patterns we will be targeting when we design your Radical Self Care daily plan of action.

Lets go back to Pain Profile 1 : Agitated Depression

Agitated Depression : these are the specific pain body messages you can experience if you are "stressed out," "burnt out" or "anxiously depressed"

Agitated Depression: Key Pain Points :

Mental : racing mind, restless, impulsive thoughts

Physical : restless, agitated, tense and edgy

Emotional : anxious, frustrated, angry

Body Language : "closed fist" : ready for fight or flight Line :

Breath Pattern : short, shallow; erratic; difficult to 'catch the breath'

Topic 2 : A TYPICAL DEPRESSION

A Typical Depression : Key Pain Points

Mental : dull dark slow

Physical : lethargic, heavy, listless, no motivation

Emotional : hopeless, helpless, sad and despairing

Body Language : "collapsed balloon" ; frozen

Breath Pattern : shallow breath, disconnected from body

Exercise : Mindful Inquiry : What about you? Which of these Pain Profiles do you most relate to?

The PNS is essential in calming and relieving the "fight or flight" response that is over-activated in burn out, depression and post traumatic stress conditions.

Lifeforce Yoga is a restorative yoga practice specifically designed to heal depression, anxiety and post traumatic stress. All of the practices found in Zen Centered : Healing your Intuitive Body are based on Lifeforce Yoga practices.

Chapter : The Secret of Unspoken Grief Trauma : Breaking the Silence

"we often hold grief at a distance, hoping to avoid our entanglement with this challenging emotion…yet this leaves us feeling detached, disconnected and cold." (From the Wild Edge of Sorrow by F. Weller)

What If We do not have to be soldiers of war to suffer the very same post traumatic stress of "battle fatigue"? mental physical exhaustion and emotional de-personalization

Big T, Little t – trauma is trauma – if our trauma response is altered or suppressed, then the little "t's" become much more damaging to our over-all health and well being. Our mental health crises suggest the lifestyles we are exposed to are hazardous to our health.

Too many of us are Suffering and in Need of Disaster Relief. But where do we find it? Look to your Body as a Source . Your Intuitive Body knows how to heal you.

Emotional mental and physical exhaustion is the core symptom of burnout, depression and post traumatic stress

As us yogis often say…, "there is no time like the present to become more present to the healing…."

Chapter : Awaken to Mindfulness of the Mind : Opening to New Awareness

Personal Narrative : *when I was at the peak of my burn out, my mind was a vicious cycle of fear filled thoughts I could not get a hold of. I truly felt like a victim of my negative thoughts and the grief they were causing me. My impossible bind ? Knowing I knew better. Now I know better. It was knowingness I was missing.*

First and foremost: mindfulness is a way of practice, a way of becoming more aware and present in the moment. It is a powerful way of training your mind to reverse the cycle of burn out by being Present in your Body in this moment in time.

Mindfulness is also an Attitude and a Viewpoint that allows you to shift from overly negative critical judgmental or punitive into a more compassionate mindset. The mindful mind is one that is able to observe with curiosity and interest in making new discoveries to better understand. Expansive consciousness allows for a creative intelligence that being "stressed out" or "burnt out" does not.

Being in the here and now. Present and attuned to your physical mental and emotional being.

The practices you will find in Zen Centered are designed to help you access this higher level of attention – Presence. You could think of Presence as a higher form of intelligence that is accessible if you choose to diverge your unconscious "comfort zone."

Zen Centered helps you choose to remember …*the Body knows how to heal you of your current state of suffering over your pain body.*

Chapter : Essential Mindful Strategies for Healthy Well Being

Topic 1 : Five Pillars of Mindfulness : Core Principles of Zen Centered

1. Learn to Pay attention
2. With an attitude of acceptance
3. Cultivate appreciation
4. Attend to with affection
5. Allow instead of expect assume or per-fect

Topic 2 : The Power of the Becoming Conscious and Aware

- Do you know that most people only use 10% of their brain's capacity?
- What about the other 90% of the brain's capacity to be creative, resourceful and access optimal potential?
- How can you learn how to tap into the insights hidden in your subconscious?

Yoga is the foundation of Zen Centered Radical Self Care for some very good reasons.

Yoga Fact :Studies conducted over the past twenty five years indicate mindfulness meditations can decrease depression, relieve anxiety, reduce fatigue, increase tolerance to stress, slow the heart rate and decrease blood pressure.

Mindfulness has also been proven to strengthen the immune system and decrease physical pain (Baer 2003, Baer, Fisher & Hass 2005, Brown, Ryan and Creswell 2007; Kabat Zinn 1991

<u>Yoga Fact</u> : Studies by Herbert Benson, M.D. at Harvard Medical School and Jon Kabat Zinn, M.D. at University of Massachusetts Medical Center have conclusively shown both yoga and meditation boost immunity and reduce stress – underlying factors in many chronic illnesses including depression and eating disorders.

As cited in the June 2011 edition of <u>Yoga Journal</u>, the practice of yoga has been shown to relax the nervous system and restore balance in the Autonomic Nervous System (ANS) between the activating, energizing, Sympathetic Nervous System (SNS) and the relaxing restorative Parasympathetic Nervous System (PNS)

<u>The Benefits of Mindfulness Practices : What Can you Look Forward to?</u> Learning to still your mind is an indispensable tool to improve your memory, sharpen intellect, increase your ability to respond to stress and even help you process negative emotions such as grief, anger and fear.

Chapter : THE SOURCE : RADICAL SELF CARE AS A SOLUTION TO BURNT OUT

<u>Personal Narrative</u> : *I have to admit…the concept of "radical" first gave me a cause to pause. The word "radical" sounded so…well… extreme – I associated it with an act of irreverence or angry rebellion. But then again when I thought more about it, the change required to get me out of my debilitated state would need to be radical and more extreme than I had become accustomed to.*

Topic 1: What Radical Self Care is and is Not

<u>Webster defines the word "radical" as "a considerable departure from the usual or the</u> traditional. I think of Radical Self Care as an extreme deviation from the norm many women – including my self – assume(d) is "acceptable" when it is an act of unhealthy tolerance – to tolerate the intolerable state of mentally emotionally and physically overly dis-stressed.

This kind of extreme deviation in thinking would tend to create widely divergent shift in existing self-view, thought habits and ways we act small in service of our false egos.

<u>Topic 1</u> : What Radical Self Care is and is not :

- ~ Radical Self Care is NOT wild and crazy or recklessly rebellious but it may be diametrically different than what you are accustomed to.
- ~ Radical Self Care is NOT ego driven selfishness – it is Body Intuitive self centeredness

Topic 2 : **the Essential Difference between Self-less ; Self-ish and Self Centered**

"What IS the difference between being self-ish and self centered?

<u>Self ish</u> ness : driven by false ego or ideals based on urgency to fill wants desires and immediately gratify self

<u>Self Centered ness</u> : driven by the Intuitive Body's awareness of what is essential and most important to healthy balance and optimal functioning

<u>Self-less-ness</u> : loss of Self identity awareness in pursuit of higher value

<u>Mindful Guide</u> : Your Body is your Source! Let your daily practices be your guide to make this distinction between what is healthy Self Care and what is not!

Topic 2: <u>Radical Self Care</u> is based on what is necessary for Whole Body Mind health and wellness. The word "radical" is a Latin for "root"

- ~ Radical Self Care is focused on what the whole body needs to be holistically healthy and balanced in wellness

<u>Topic 3: Radical Self Care Practices</u> are grounded in Ancient Medicines that are Holistically oriented to heal into Wholeness. We look to sources of ancient healing traditions and nature based remedies.

Radical self care is not complicated, it is more about how to keep things simple by observing what is innate – or natural to the biological organism!

When you focus on using the Mind to Observe, you can engage with curiosity not overly critical ideals. You are free to Prioritize the health of your Intuitive Body without unnecessary stress or undue suffering.

what a radical concept to become mindfully Present to.

Chapter : Radical Self Care as a Form of Compassion

<u>Topic 1 : Radical Self Care is based in Respect and Reverence : Back to "the body is precious…." Buddha</u>

1. Be your Own Best Friend Forever instead of your own worst frenemy!
2. Be Unconditional in your Compassion for Self (and Others)let go of false beliefs and romanticized idealism and false ego pursuits
3. Be Absolute in your compassion and your courage
   - ~ to do what at first might seem Radical!
4. Be focused on what is your Best Self

- Let go of the over idealized "perfect" be you – not a carbon copy fantasy image that only exists in a virtual world of "the photoshopped feminine"

Compassionate AND Courageous Self Care : A Radical antidote to Burnt out, Stressed out and Psychosomatically dis-stressed!

Can you take a leap of faith into your courage? What would it take for you to…" return to rest of sentence "seek a radical antidote to Burnt Out.etc.

Zen Centered is my way of saying we do not need to accept stress as any kind of "norm" or tolerate living in secret distress.

because your Body can heal the source of suffering when you use simple holistic medicines and practice what I am calling, Zen Centered Radical Self Care.

Just like I did.

You can too.

AWAKEN

"the thought manifests as the word; the word manifests as the deed; the deed develops into a habit. Watch your thought and its way with care and let it spring from love born out of concern for ALL beings." Buddha

<u>The Body is a Miracle</u> : Yes, your body is a miracle, a mystery and a source of magic in its ability to heal and restore essential balance.

<u>Inspiring Vision of What's Possible</u> : What is possible with Radical Self Care

<u>Five New Ways to Awaken</u> :

1. <u>The Body IS Precious</u> ; fragile yet resilient and miraculous in all of the mysterious ways it works to keep your mental emotional and physical well being in balance. There is an inherent beauty and grace in how the parts work together in harmony and are greater than the sum of their individual parts. Especially so when we take good care of our selves in simple yet essential ways.

2. <u>The Body IS a Messenger</u> ; think of symptoms are signals of inner imbalance causing dis-stress ; the body creates symptoms for a reason; for every symptom there is a mind body cause and effect – either positive or negative

3. <u>The Body is a Miracle</u> : your body is capable of not only resting and restoring but revitalizing your body and mind to expand into your personal best.

4. <u>Your Body is a Temple</u> . If you could picture your body as a temple, what would your temple look like? How would you see your self treating your body with reverence in your rituals? Would you say grace or pray for spiritual guidance or anoint your skin with essential oils?

5. <u>The Body is the Engine of Your Machine</u> what if you thought of how your body has its own GPS and Awareness Panel to signal SOS – engine needs oil, tire needs air or time for a 50,000 mile tune up? Do you let your car run on empty without assuming it will stop working for you?

<u>Chapter : How to Reverse the cycle of Pain from Pain Body to Intuitive Body by practicing Zen Centered Radical Self Care.</u>

NEXT STEPS TO REVERSE BURN OUT :

1. Take a Compassionate Inventory
2. Identify Key Secret Pain Points
3. Identify Key Burn Out Pain Patterns

Focus on simple holistic medicines to remedy the pain of your Intuitive Body

1. Mindfulness as Medicine
2. Yoga as Medicine
3. Plants as Medicine

Zen Centered Radical Self Care starts here with the intention to:

- Be conscious
- Be present
- Be curious
- Make mindful inquiries about what else is possible?

How do you do this, you ask?

Thank you for asking, mindful one….let us begin to continue…

Chapter : Healing with Intuitive Body Wisdom

Opening Story : What is possible if I believe My Body is A Source of Wisdom

- Topic 1 : How can my Body Heal me if I treat my Self like I truly Matter?
- Topic 2 : What would my BFF say? How would she support me in changing my Pain Patterns?
- Topic 3 : How does your Self Talk shift if you are Mindful of being your own BFF?

~   Exercise : Mindfulness Mind Meditation : Loving Kindness : me
     and my BFF Body Parts

Chapter : Yoga is Medicine for the Body and the Mind

What is Yoga but a union of the body and the mind and the spirit?

Topic : Healing Remedies for Disaster Relief : The Scientific Research

As a professor of psychiatry at New York Medical College, Patricia
Gerbarg seized the opportunity to test whether yoga could help tsunami
survivors in India. The tsunami in 2004 that ripped through Southeast
Asia brought with it a tidal wave of psychic devastation. The depression
and post traumatic stress that ravaged many residents of the coastal villages
from India to Indonesia provided a living laboratory for testing the most
powerful cures available.

Mindful Inquiry : am I my own worst enemy?

Second line : Mindful Journal Writing Exercise : write a dialogue
between you and your own worst enemy ; then write a dialogue between
you and your Intuitive Body as Best Friend Forever.

Write out the new promise into an affirmative meditation and a daily self
talk ritual.

What wound up providing the best help to some of the most afflicted
survivors? Yoga.

Patricia Gerbarg's research with yoga and ptsd survivors validates other
scientific studies that teach us : When you change your breathing pattern,
you can change your emotions." Gerbarg's studies have found that yogic
breathing physiologically affects the nervous system to produce profound
changes in emotional states.

The miracle of yoga? It is both a discipline and a tool that heals and restores your Body's innate ability to guide you with intuition into a state of awareness often called "knowingness."

Chapter : Be Intentional: Shift into Intuitive Body Beliefs through Daily Practices

<u>Personal Narrative</u> *Once I let go of feeling so angry I wasn't able to heal in a "conventional way," I began to relax and reconnect to my intuition about what is essential for my healthy recovery.*

<u>Topic 1 : Setting a Daily Intention</u> or a "sankalpa" to guide and support your vision of Radical Self Care to heal your Intuitive Body

Practice Zen Centered practices to access wisdom of yoga principle of "sankalpa" or the power of setting an Intention. Use your Mind to see and then say what is possible

<u>Topic 2</u> : Patanjali's eight limbs of yoga offers simple principles to practice in the here and now. Here are four we focus on here :

(1) what you do

(2) what you notice when you do it

(3) what you accept is yours to change and what is not

(4) what action you take to create desired change

<u>Topic 3: The daily practice of intentional restorative yoga</u> builds the discipline or the fire to motivate momentum – this is called "tapas". The more you practice, the more you fuel the fire of dedicated disciplines..

Radical Self Care Practices : If I operate from the Intuitive Body Premise - "My Body is the Engine of My Machine," what then are the Daily Practice choices that will fuel my engine?

Chapter : Be Unconditional yet Accountable in Daily Practice

Personal Narrative : *When I let go of control freaking my recovery and allowed my body to guide me, things moved forward. Once I could admit that my "machismo" approach to the problem AND conventional medicines were failing me, I recalled the wisdom of following my own best advice. I remembered what I had learned from yoga about how to release the illusions of control I become attached to. I recall the wisdom of my own advice, "what would buddha say?"*

Topic 1 : Radical self Care = Do no Harm : Challenge the Pain Belief Patterns of "no pain no gain"

Topic 2 : Radical Self Care = Compassionate Self Care: let go of running on empty

Topic 3 : Radical Self Care = Unconditional But Accountable : be your new BFF and treat your self accordingly

Exercise : Journal : Be your Own BFF : Write a letter to your Intuitive Body as if she is your BFF and you are making her a new promise.

Chapter : The Power of Intention

"Act as if what you do makes a difference. Because it does." William James

Under normal conditions, you will notice how your mind and thoughts are diffused. The power of resolve focuses and concentrates your thoughts and increases your minds innate capacities for expanded creative intelligence. "Sankalpa" is the Sanskrit word for resolve or intention – a focal point to awaken the latent power of the mind and allow us to become more capable and resourceful in our actions.

When applied methodically, sankalpa empowers the mind to lead us to new heights, ones to which an unfocused mind or one that lacks resolve is simply incapable of doing. Resolution increases our capacity to discern and take specific actions necessary to manifest the results we desire. Recent scientific research proves that our intentions have the power to affect our future.

Topic: In the yoga sutras, "practice" is defined as a "sustained effort" to be "there." Doing something consistently with love and reverence cultivates mastery over one's mind that reveals that highest state of human experience.

Topic 3 : In his book, The Relaxation Response, Dr. Herbert Benson describes how he had his patients focus on ONE word and do nothing but that one word for a period of time each day. If other thoughts started to distract them, they were to simply shift their mind to refocus on that one word. His patients reported a significant decrease in blood pressure and muscle tension from this one simple exercise.

Exercise Practice : Just Say Ommmmmm : a simple sound like "om" can act as a mantra that links into the auditory sensory awareness to enhance the relaxing effects of your meditation practice.

So Hom Meditation : Sit in a comfortable well supported upright position or if you prefer, lie down. Close your eyes and begin to tune into the sound of your breath. Imagine the inhale breath makes a "so" sound and the exhale breath makes a "hum" sound. As the breath comes in through your nostrils, hear in your mind "sooooooo" for the entire duration of the inhalation ; pause before you exhale into the sound "hummmmmmmm" for the length of the exhalation. If your attention wavers, simply return your focus on the sound of your breath. Begin again with inhaling to the "sooooo" sound and expanding into the "hummmmmm" sound as you exhale. Start with two minutes and build up to five minutes. Remain quietly observing what you notice about how you feel in your body and your mind.

Chapter : A Balance of Ease and Effort

"your practice must be mindful of your goal while consistently endeavoring to achieve it." Patanjali

GET better ACQUAINTED WITH YOUR INTUITIVE BODY

- ~ Five sensory Awarenesses : Five Sensible Senses
- ~ The Felt Sense
- ~ The Body in Nature
- ~ Intuition or Knowingness
- ~ Insight not Intellect

Chapter : Zen Centered Principle and Essential Practice : Intentional Breath

"breath is the pulse of the mind"

Breath is the foundation of any and all healing yoga practices. I see too many yoga videos focus more on form and less on the movement of breath. Zen Centered Radical Self Care practices are always based on an active pranayama practice. "Prana" is lifeforce.

Pure energy.

"Pranayama" is an intentional way of channeling this lifeforce energy to the benefit of your body mind and spirit. Most of us are barely conscious of our breathing habits – yet once we become more conscious, we are already beginning to build a bridge of healing awareness.

Pranayama is one of the most important tools in yoga practice. Prana is considered to be the "lifeforce energy" and is the equivalent of "chi" in Chinese medicines. Pranayama, or intentional breath practice, is the cornerstone of Zen Centered Radical Self Care daily practices.

Ancient yogis learned consciously controlled breath patterned practices has profound effects on the Nervous System. They understood that by using their bodies to relax their minds, they could calm what they called "the fluctuations" of the mind.

From a yogic perspective, breathing in dysfunctional ways can be both a consequence and a cause of stress; you may breathe erratically when you feel stress AND choppy, shallow breath causes tension and unease.

You can immediately reverse this unhealthy cycle and defuse the stress response when you focus on : (1) slowing the breath

(2) deepening the breath;

(3) expanding the inhalations, the exhalations and the suspensions in between.

Mindful Breath Practice : This can be as simple as taking ten seconds now to notice the rhythm of your breath. Notice how you can pause between the inhale and the exhale breath.

Chapter : Mindful Practice : Just Breathe : Tune in to Where you are

By selectively focusing your attention on internal phenomenon like the breath, you can learn to tune out external phenomena. You can still hear the din of outside noise but it fades into the quietude of the background.

Mindful Breath Practice : Compare Busy with Quiet

Chapter : The Power of Prana to Create a Bridge between Body and Mind

Science supports our practice! Research shows that deep yogic breath acts on the vagus nerve – the 'rest and digest' response – or the calming pathway of the autonomic nervous system (PNS) that extends from the BRAIN stem to the abdomen.

When the vagus nerve is activated, it helps to automatically slow down breathing and heart rate and increases intestinal activity. The vagus nerve not only carries signals from the brain to the body but ferries signals from the body back to the brain.

Mindful Awareness Prompt : Becoming Aware of the Breath IS an Act of Mindfulness

Chapter : The Power of Prana : Just Breathe ! Tune into the Rhythm of your Breath

The Sanskrit word "prana" translates into "life force energy" or what is also known as "chi"

According to ancient yogic teachings, the left nostril is connected to "ida" an energy pathway or "nadi" that travels alongside the spine. "Ida" is cooling, restorative and feminine in nature and corresponds to "yin" in traditional Chinese medicine.

The right nostril is governed by "pingala, a complementary nadi that is warming, energizing and masculine, roughly the equivalent to "yang"

Left Nostril Breathing : cooling and restorative in nature

1. Stimulates relaxation response
2. Stimulates the right hemisphere of the brain
3. Lowers blood sugar levels

4. Decreases heart rate

Right Nostril Breathing : warming and energizing in nature

5. Stimulates the fight or flight response
6. Stimulates the left hemisphere of the brain
7. Increases verbal performance
8. Increases blood sugar levels
9. Increases heart rate

Scientific studies show that the nasal breathing cycle naturally alternates between left and right nostril breathing for periods ranging from a few minutes to a few hours.

This pattern can be shifted with intentional breathing practices like Right Nostril Vitality Breath, Left Nostril Calming Breath and Alternate Nostril Breath Guided Practice.

Simple Breath Practice Awareness : Take a deep breath, lifting the rib cage. Letting go of the breath, let the shoulders drop while the spine stays gently in place.

Allow your mind to rest on the image of a mountain and a river running through it. Just breathe and notice what you notice.

Notice how you embody the strength of the mountain as your breath is the river that runs through it.

Chapter : Balance of Effort and Ease

The Ancient Sage, Patanjali, suggests we focus on a Balance of Ease and Effort.

How balanced is your ease to effort scale?

The answer lies within.

<u>Exercise : Mindfulness Practice : Practice Doing No-thing-ness</u>

1. Go horizontal. Settle in til your body feels fully supported by the surface you are resting upon.

   Next rest one hand on your tummy and the other hand on your heart.

   Listen to the beat of your heart beneath your hand as your belly gently rises and falls into the rhythm of your breath.

   Breathe smoothly. Slowly. Deeply.

   Relax into the rhythm of your breath rising into your heart space and relaxing into your back as you exhale slowly.

   Smoothly. Deeply.

   Do no-thing-more-than-this for the next five minutes. Or more.

   It's okay if you lost track of time.

   Relax. Trust. Your body's got this.

<u>Exercise : Guided Prana Flow : Breath Awareness :</u>

1. Intention: during asana, focus more on what you are doing with your breath than on your muscles and bones
2. notice what you notice about what happens to the BREATH when the pose is easy for you
3. Next notice what you notice about what happens to the BREATH when the pose is difficult?

Chapter : The Power of the Mindful Mind to Observe : Learn from the Five Senses and the Felt Sense

The "felt sense" or internal body sensations serve as a portal of awareness and enhance your awareness beyond the five senses. This deepens your connection with the Intuitive Body because in a very real way the felt sense IS the Intuitive Body. The felt sense can be influenced by thought – yet it is a feeling not a thought.

Emotions contribute to the felt sense but the felt sense is much more nuanced, subtle and intricate than the intense direct feeling of joy sorrow anger or fear. The felt sense is sometimes vague, always complex and ever changing. It is moving, shifting and transforming constantly.

The physical (external) senses of sight, sound, smell, touch and taste are elements that contribute to only a portion of what becomes the foundation for the experience of the felt sense. Other important data includes the positions the body takes, the tensions it has, the movements it makes the overall temperature of the body, etc.

The Intuitive Body : The Power of the "Felt Sense" = Instinctive Resonance

1. Innate wisdom = felt sense
2. Body intuitions: the process of being consciously aware of your body and sensations makes any experience more somatically intense
3. The felt sense is not a mental experience but a physical one.
4. The felt Sense is a bodily awareness of a situation or a person or an event
5. The Felt Sense relays experience instead of the mind which interprets the experience

Mindful Experience : The Felt Sense in Practice :

1. When we Observe both closely and at a distance, the individual sensations can be experienced simultaneously to integrate the experience.

2. Enhanced awareness is the physical externals - like sight sound smell touch taste - plus the body's internal awareness of the positions it takes, the movement it makes the tensions it has and the temperature, etc.
3. Awareness is experiencing what is present without trying to change or interpret it
4. Observe and describe the physiologic sensations you are experiencing
5. Sensation is the physical phenomena that contributes to our overall experience

Chapter : How does your Mind Interpret Sensation?

As you begin to observe through your daily practice, you will notice how Internal body sensation serves as a portal through which we can find the symptoms. Because symptoms are blocked energy, we can notice where our body feels tense tight and blocked.

By increasing Awareness through ZC practice, present and intentional breath can unbind and free trapped emotional energies. The Felt Sense encompasses the clarity, instinctual power and fluidity necessary to heal and transform the Pain Body.

Mindful Guided PracTice : Body Scan : Felt sense Awareness Exercise :

Notice the nuances in your sensations :

1. Begin by noticing your arms and legs and what you feel where your limbs make contact with the surface that support you.
2. Sense into your skin and notice the way your clothes feel.
3. Sense underneath your skin – what sensations are there?
4. Now gently remembering these sensations, how do you know that you feel comfortable? What physical sensations contribute to the overall feeling of comfort?

5. Does becoming aware of these sensation make you feel more or less comfortable? Does this change over time?
6. Sit for moment and fully enjoy the sensations

The Five Sensible Senses :

Pay attention with all of your Five Senses. Use Mindful Inquiries to connect – Ask :

- What do I see?
- What do I hear?
- What is the scent?
- What is the texture?
- If there was a taste would it be bitter or sweet or savory?

Exercise : Practice : Counting on your Five Senses :

1. What are five colors I can see?
2. What are four sounds I can hear?
3. What are three scents I can smell?
4. What are two textures I feel on my skin – cool warm soft silky or rough
5. What is one taste I taste on my tongue? Is it bitter or sweet or savory?

Mindfulness : The Center of your Practice

Chapter : Cultivating Stillness : The Power of the Meditative Mind

The process of tuning in to your Intuitive Body begins with Learning to still your mind; this does not require you to be a master of meditation before you even begin to practice the tools that cultivate stillness. It is through the daily practice of becoming Mindful in your daily practice that you will develop the skill and mastery of the mindful mind. The practice of mindfulness is a work in progress – which will be progressive as you dedicate your self to Radical Self Care of the mind.

Topic 1 : Stillness is the seat of intuition, where source begins and ends. Deep calm and ease are the state that allows you to move beyond the limitations of the intellect and the irrational rational mind. Mindfulness allows you to observe without making false assumptions about what is under your control and what is not.

Topic 2 : The practice of meditation was developed by the ancient sages to free the mind from its normally distracted state and to make it more capable of seeing what it ordinarily does not see. Ancient yogi masters relied on the movements of yoga poses and postures to access their capacity to slow the "fluctuations of the mind." These early yogi masters realized their capacity to build new "samskaras" or what scientists today call "neural pathways," through their daily yoga and meditation practices.

Many of the benefits of meditation are now recognized in clinical research and widely documented but it is only in your own practice you will truly discover you own innate potential. Ultimately, the process of learning to still your mind through meditation is a portal to a completely different way of thinking and feeling.

Topic 3: Meditation is an antidote to the way most of us use our brains in the digital age. We live in a time of sensory overload and despite all our technological advances, most of us feel like we are running out of time so we do as many things possible.

Multitasking has been shown to impair cognitive skills like attention short and long term memory, processing speed, visual and auditory processing, logic and reasoning!

The long term effect is our brain can literally atrophy parts of our brain and impair our brains optimal functioning!

Meditation does the opposite. Mindfulness meditations shift your brain into a more balanced state of active and restorative to heal your body mind.

The Power of the Mindful Mind : Expansive Awareness

1. Concentration or Dharana – this is the ability to maintain clarity and focus despite distractions
2. Meditation or Dhyana – this is a relaxed concentration where the stream of thoughts in the mind slows.
3. Blissful Absorption or Samadhi – this is the state of mind of absolute attention with no interrupting thoughts

Miracles in Healing

The Body Heals the Mind : The Mind Heals the Body

THE MINDFUL MIND : THE POWER OF PERCEPTION

"perception is projection"

Chapter : A Matter of Perception : Is it a Pain Problem or a Suffering Problem

<u>Personal Narrative :</u>*When I stopped believing in thoughts like "my back is killing me" or "my neck is on fire," I could use my own wisdom to heal with simple holistic tools like the Pain Intensity Scale (PINs) so I could measure my pain in ways that did not depress me – then use tools like palming or tapping to defuse the sensations! I could use essential oils to heal soothe and comfort and heal the pain in my neck and back."*

<u>Topic 1 : Pain and suffering are not the same.</u> Pain is a temporary sensation, a physical response to injury. Temporary sensations come and go. The sensation may be persistent or pervasive but sensation does not remain permanent! nor do repressed sensation need to become sources of psychosomatic illnesses.

"The root of all suffering is attachment."

<u>Pain is a temporary Sensation not a state of mind you need to suffer in</u>

<u>Topic 2 : Suffering is a state of mind.</u> The intellect can interpret – or misinterpret – what the sensation means and how we respond – or react – to the circumstance or situation we are in.

When we become attached to unconscious beliefs, we may be acting without thinking in a way that does the Intuitive Body more harm than good. We can become attached to acting as if we are not in pain when we are sick and tired and miserable. We can become attached to distractions and multi tasking to avoid feeling empty or nervous or depressed about our mother is dying of cancer.

We may become chronically dis-stressed with mysterious aches and pains that become even more mysterious psychosomatic medical conditions or categories.

Topic 3 : Uncover Pain Beliefs and Pain Patterns :

What are the Pain beliefs that drive you? Pain Patterns & Negativity Beliefs as Reinforcers : Here are some examples to draw from. You can add or subtract from this list to come up with your own Top Three Pain Beliefs. Remember, a belief is an idea or a cluster of ideas you are deeply emotionally attached to.

- No Pain No Gain!
- Image is Everything
- Fake it til you Make it
- Grin and bear it even if you're sick tired and miserable

Topic 3 : Make Meaningful Connections between What you Think What you Feel ad What you Do

Exercise : Mindful Inquiry : Link the Pain Belief with what you do, how you feel and what you think:

1. What do I Do in response?
2. How does the pain Belief DRIVE me (what is the number 1-10 ?)
3. What do i think in response?
4. What are the feelings that go with this?

Journal your Pain Body Belief Narrative : what is the cause and the consequence of your Pain Body Beliefs?

1. How does this belief serve me well?
2. What feelings go with the belief alternative?
3. What would it take for me to change the way I think about this?
4. What would the positive negative consequence be when I do?

"You are your thoughts …everything you do rises from what you think…."
Buddha

Chapter : Inventory : A Matter of Perception : Is it a Pain Problem or a Suffering Problem of the Mind

"The root of all suffering is attachment."

Pain is a temporary physical response to injury. Suffering is a problem of the mind, the beliefs and daily habits that drive you.

When you are ready to let go of suffering in pain body beliefs and habits, use the tool of Mindful Review. There is no time like the Present to discover a non critical but essential review to transform how you heal your pain.

Chapter : Uncover Pain Beliefs and Pain Patterns :

What are the Pain beliefs that drive you?

1. Pain Patterns & Negativity Beliefs as Reinforcers
2. How do we Heal these pain patterns with Zen Centered?

Mindful practice : Practice the art of Observation and notice what you notice without making any critical judgments assumptions or otherwise interpreting. Make note of what you notice to further reflect upon in later review.

Mindful Awareness : Creative Journal : Uncovering Patterns

"it's not what you see but how you see it"

Using a journal to make notes, focus on the follow observations:

1. What are my primary pain belief attachments?
2. How do these Pain Beliefs drive my thoughts, feelings and actions?

Mindful Mind Body Scan

This is a powerful tool to integrate with the use of a Mindful Review practice, such as the one you just did in Reviewing Pain Body Beliefs.

Mindful Review allows you to notice where in your body you carry the pain sensations; the Mindful Mind Body Scan relief tool helps you release your body from carrying the pain of how you think and what you believe.

Chapter : The Power of New Paradigms : Zen Centered : The Intuitive Body

"when you change the way you look at things, things change" Wayne Dyer

Topic 1 : The Power of What you Believe :

Mindful Inquiry : Consider the Possibilities

How would it make a difference if you truly believed….my Body is a Miracle?

What if you believe "My Body is a Temple? What would you choose to do instead of what you do now?

Topic 2 : Intuitive Body Beliefs :

1. My Body is a Miracle
2. My Body is a Temple of Divine Presence
3. My Body is a Source of Innate Strength
4. My Body is a Source of Intuitive Wisdom

<u>Topic 3 : Cause and Effect</u> : What would be the positive consequence ?

Write Examples of Radical Self Care actions and feelings that go with above four belief sets.

1. What would I do different?
2. How would I feel different?
3. What thoughts would I have about this difference?
4. What are the thoughts feelings or beliefs that block me from believing I can change this?

The Problem of Burn Out : Lost Connections

<u>Zen Centered Healing Remedy</u> : Get Back to Nature to Reconnect in Body Mind and Spirit

Rediscover The power of stillness to heal profound darkness of the soul. Recall how Nature can be a safe refuge for a broken spirit.

When is the last time you spent time in Nature?

THE TRUE NATURE OF HEALING

"…silence beckons when we gaze upon a …mountain until our concerns begin to vanish, our desires and ego thin to nothing and our sense of where we end …begins dissolves."

Personal Narrative: *the only way I got through the worst of my depression was through the force of my Intuitive Body. She literally commanded my physical being to walk out the door of darkness into the morning sun light where nature could warm the coldness of my numb frozen heart. Somehow my death wish loosened its grip so I could heal more with hope.*

MINDFULNESS : THE CENTER OF YOUR PRACTICE

Mindful Inquiry : Mindful Review : Tune in to Where you are

Intentional Restorative Focus :

By focusing your attention on Restorative practices, you can both calm the SNS and activate the PNS.

This is a simple yet powerful intention that allows you to stay aligned with the healing interests and energies of the Intuitive Body.

A powerful Zen Centered principle I learned in my LFY therapy trainings, is to "meet your self where you are."

This is Not the same as where your mind thinks you should be or could be. Where you are physically mentally and emotionally in this present moment?

If you find you draw a blank, take a deep breath.

Relax.

Let Zen Centered guide you.

we consider any time spent with Nature a Restorative practice and one of the simplest ways to begin again.

Chapter : Reverse Pattern of Go Go Go : Go Slow Motion

<u>Opening Story</u> : *I can see now that my prolonged period of physical recovery was the only way I could stop to slow down. Because of the nature of my back and neck injury, I had no choice but to pace myself and gradually return from horizontal with restorative yoga practices and a ten minute walk outside in nature.*

Topic 1: <u>Respect your Body's Need to Heal Resistance</u> with Respect and Insightful Boundary Awareness

- ~ Ease into a new practice.
- ~ Learn how to pace your self instead of push push push.

Topic 2 : <u>When is a Limit Not a Limitation</u>? What if you think of a physical resistance as an opportunity to explore where you are free and where you need to set a safety limit to avoid injury?

- ~ When is a limit not a limitation but an opportunity to explore how to let go of resistance and safely release?
- ~ When is a limit a way of avoiding injury and building strength and flexibility?
- ~ How could strength and flexibility serve you into health and wellness?

<u>Topic 3</u> : <u>Notice How Limits are Not Limitations</u> but help you Set Priority

- ~ If your Body is the engine of your machine, notice how you can pump the brakes and just like you can press the metal to the floor.
- ~ When is it time to slow down and ease off the accelerator?

Exercise : <u>Mindful Journal Inquiry</u> : The follow series of inquiries will help you focus your thoughts and writing intentions. You can choose to answer some or all of the questions but take time to reflect on the question before you begin to journal the answer. Then let the pen flow freely.

<u>Mindful Inquiries</u> :

1. Where in your life do you need to "heed your need for speed?"
2. If you could adopt a new creed, "no need to speed" where would you slow down to avoid crashing and burning your health?
3. What is the catalyst, the cause and the consequence of your need for speed?

Chapter : Essential components of Radical Self Care Dailies

<u>Opening Story</u> : *The only way to get on with the healing was to get on with the healing practices. Daily. Not later in the day or tomorrow. But in the Now. This Present moment. Take a pause to breathe …smoothly slowly and deeply. Simple as that. Repeat. Until I find the rhythm of my breath begins to flow*

Remember all Radical Self Care is based on respect and reverence for how the Body is a miracle and the engine of your machine.

What are the basic essential ingredients needed to fuel the engine of your machine?

Simple holistic medicines to remedy the pain relationship you are in with your Body. If we are burnt out or depressed, we may have lost our appetite and forget the essential truth – Fuel your Body with Quality Fuels.

Do you run your car engine on empty?

Do you put toxic fuel in your car and expect it to go anywhere without crashing and burning?

Topic 1: Mindfulness as Medicine

- How will you practice Mindfulness of the Mind as one of your top priorities?
- What Zen Centered practices will you choose to be part of your daily Radical Self Care plan?

Topic 2 : Movement as Medicine

- What morning practice will you choose to start the day out with your Intuitive Body as priority?
- If movement is something to choose throughout the day, how will you move out of sedentary inactive or frozen in autopilot?
- What evening practice will you choose to end the day so you can relax into a deep restorative sleep?

Topic 3 Plants as Medicine

- Choose whole foods to fuel the body mind with essential nutrition to boost the brain's mood chemistry**
- Choose herbs and nutraceuticals to help rebalance a depleted brain chemistry*
- Choose to relieve pain with plant botanicals which include essential oils, exfoliators and skin cremes to renew and revitalize your skin.

*See the book "How to Use Herbs, nutrients and Yoga in Mental Health Care by P. Gerbarg et al

**See the Mindfully Mediterranean Food Guide for more information on healthy holistic nutrition including essential foods, meal plans and recipe guides

Chapter : Radical Self Care Dailies : Set your Intentions

Exercise : Set Daily Intentions to Include the Above In your Radical Self Care Plan of Healing Action

Defining your Dailies : What and How to Do Radical Self Care for your Intuitive Body

Mindful Inventory : Use Journal To Define and Track : Whole Plant Foods as Medicine for the Health of the Intuitive Body

Mindful Review : What whole plant based foods are you including in your Daily Nutrition Plan?

1. Foods I already include to Power Boost my Body :
2. Foods I need to Add In to Boost my Nutrition :
3. Food stuffs fake foods or toxic food products I need to eliminate

Mindful Inventory : Movement as Medicine for the Pain Body and Mind

1. Movement I already do
2. Movement I need to include
3. Unhealthy exercise or no exercise habits I need to eliminate :

Chapter : Back to Nature : Holistic medicines that respect the whole body mind and spirit

Topic : Healing Remedies = Natural Medicine approach to focus on what is healing not what is a miracle cure.

Topic : Mindfulness and Meditations - not Medications - to still the mind

Topic : Nature plus Nurture = Radical Self Care

"many of us sense that we are afflicted with a basic deprivation. Through constraints of time and modern stress, we often find ourselves feeling separated – as if by a glass wall – from nature, from others and even from the silent enchantment of our own being." (The Independent, J. Powell)

In our chronically distracted state of mind and autopilot over do do doing, we may have forgotten how fundamentally nourishing silence is to our souls. We may even disparage the contemplative impulse as folly or foolishness to be disregard. It is the opposite. Who first said, "silence is golden?"

BACK TO NATURE

"Nature is the art of god"

Personal Narrative : *"…deep in the forest, my senses became sharper, I could feel the warm air on my cool skin and the hair on the back of my neck as the breeze whispered all around me. I could feel my body release the tension that gripped ahold of my heart and my head.*

In Nature, we become more present in our bodies. We shift our rhythm to align with that of Mother Nature. We become one with Source.

Safe Refuges to Retreat Into

We are here to help you remember the wisdom of Ancient science learned from the natural world.

Retreat centers are places of the infinite and the sacred. A sacred retreat is a safe place where we commune with both private and collective solitudes. A retreat center both nourishes our vision and allows for our souls to expand and open. A retreat center safely shelters us in the most intimate textures of serenity and silence.

They allow us to dream and transcend into peace, while we readjust our pace. Their nooks and corners offer themselves as centers of simplicity and safety. Sequestered securely within their folds, we experience the primitiveness of refuge. We feel safe to open to pure Being.

This is your Source, your Zen Center.

Nature is your portal to the infinite and the sacred.

Meditative Silence bestows upon us a blessed distance from the noise, the pressure and demands of the modern day world.

"Contemplative silence transcends thought." (from J. Powell, University of California Santa Barbara)

Yogi master, Patanjali speaks of the importance of cultivating a tranquil mind through meditations, self reflections and contemplation. This is the path to the true sense of contentment we hunger and thirst for. Notice how contentment is not the same as the pursuit of "happy" but may be even more fulfilling to our soul and spirit.

Ever present and dwelling in the heart of every creature is an innermost self. It is only through a stilled mind she can be known. She is the self who teaches each living creature *to attain perfection according to her own nature.*

This is your Zen Centered challenge to fulfill this purpose and promise : seek the wisdom of your Intuitive Body to attain perfection according to your own unique human nature.

Exercise Practice : Illustrative Journal : Illustrate your Serene Scene where you can find peace and tranquility here…and now in this present moment. This is a place where the uniqueness of your human nature is free to grow through the seasons of your life so far. This is a safe and sacred place for your new beginning. Begin to draw your Safe Place in Nature Scene with all five of your senses engaged and actively represented on the page.

Chapter : Return to the Essential : Nurture with Nature

"Nature is always teaching us who we are meant to be" (from <u>The Four Desires</u>, by Rod Stryker)

Nature reminds us how our Intuitive voice is always omnipresent. We need not strive or drive to seek more more more more. We can simply choose to Be. Because in the time we spend with Nature, it is one of those times and places where we can tune in with less effort and more ease.

<u>Mindful Inquiry : Mindful Recall</u> : Can you remember how this is true for you? Recall a memory from your past when you felt the power and presence of being at one with mother nature?

<u>The Wisdom of Yogis</u> : The ancient sage, Patanjali reminds us that for our Intuition to grow as a force in our lives, we must learn to honor it. In the Yoga Sutras, a reverent practice is defined as a sustained effort to be "there" – the place of stillness and mastery over one's mind that reveals the highest state of human experience. Zen Centered Radical Self Care is based on Cultivating Respect and Reverence ; and can be reflected in the practices you choose to begin. Set your priorities accordingly.

Consider your reverent practice a mirror of what you learn from the Natural World about stillness and the beauty of healing in grace.

Chapter : Integrated daily Practices : The Nature of Healing Holistically

<u>Personal Narrative</u> : *At the worse of my depression, I recall the moments when I could do nothing more than listen to the sound of Mother Nature reflecting back life in her sounds of stillness. It took everything I had to bring my self out of my cocoon of darkness to sit in the Presence of Mother Nature. Of course I realize now, this was my Intuitive Body commanding me to heal where my intellect failed me.*

Stillness filled my soul with the something that had been missing. The healing light the sun cast against the flickering shadows where I could feel my skin warm again. I hadn't even realized how frozen in my sorrow I had become.

Since Zen Centered Is not yoga only : Yoga is only the portal into your Intuitive Body – but not the only portal.

One of the best ways to tune back in is to retreat into nature.

So let us begin, let us return to the Source – Mother Nature. Simply listen in her stillness. Look forward to getting reacquainted with your Intuitive Body.

<u>Simple yet Essential :</u>

<u>Mindful Daily Wellness Practice</u>: Take a daily walk in nature and illustrate it in your Mindfulness Journal. Let go of logical mind pursuits, get back in touch with the simple and basic.

Chapter : The power of infinite wonder. Reverence within the Natural World

True States of natural beauty and grace. In our modern day culture so heavily saturated with technology, we have lost our essential connection to mother earth and need to restore renew and replenish our Authentic Self there. Most of us spend 90% of our time indoors.

<u>TURN TO SOURCE : LET NATURE BE YOUR GUIDE</u>

1. <u>Mindfulness as a Walking Practice</u> : Mindful Walk in Nature
2. <u>Be Present</u> : Pay attention to your Body and how it feels when your feet touch the ground, when the breeze cools your sun warmed skin.
3. <u>Illustrative Journaling</u> : Carry a small notebook with you in your pocket. After ten minutes, find a quiet place where you can

reflect illustrate and write in your Journal . Focus on the 5 sensory awarenesses with words and images you are drawn to .

Pay Attention : Be Intentional : Notice how it feels different to Sit beneath a tree than to stand by the surf and Walk barefoot in the meadow. Write these insights in your journal and draw a picture of the tree, the surf and the meadow

Sit beneath a tree

Sit by the surf

Walk barefoot in the meadow.

Do yoga in nature.

In the natural world.

Reconnect with movement.

Body.

Breath.

In Nature we become more present with our physical bodies. We shift our biorhythm to tune in to the energies of the natural world. Notice how it feels to be Present and aware of how you feel in your body – your feet on the ground, your heart beating with the rhythm of your breath and the sun on your skin and the wind in your hair.

Mindful Mind : Mantra to Focus the Mind : Mantra is a simple sound or phrase to help focus the busy mind as you are becoming more Present with each step you take.

Simple Mantra: Breath is the bridge between the mind and the body.

Simple Mantra : Earth Water Fire Air

Simple Mantra : Body Like Earth : Mind Like Sky : Breath Like Wind

Mindful Journal : Make notes of your observations. Notice what you notice about how you feel physically mentally and emotionally : make notes here:

EMBODY NATURE'S WISDOM

What can you Learn from Mother Nature about how to be Present? Observe with a curious mind :

1. Have you ever noticed the way a tree holds space?
   - It is surrendered in a state of grace.
2. Trees hold a timeless beauty we can all embrace.
   - Embrace her beauty with all of your five sense now
3. Walk amongst the trees and breathe slowly deeply until your breath is smooth and rhythmic
   - Let go into the feelings of surrender

Zen Centered Radical Self Care Intentional Practice : OUTSIDE IN

Mindful inquiry : How can you bring the beauty of nature indoors?

1. Bring flowers greens and other objects found in nature to create an altar or a zen center for you to retreat to
2. Next Create a collage with pictures and images of places in nature that inspire you
3. choose theme music to calm soothe and inspire self reflection
4. choose botanicals and floral essences to scent the room
5. Next Create an altar in your Zen Zone as a daily ritual.

Essential Healing : Yoga is Restorative Sleep Practices

Essential Restorative Sleep :

If you are suffering from burn out, chances are your sleep patterns are erratic or disrupted. One of the core symptoms of any psychosomatic illnesses is insomnia and is a top priority to target with any Radical Self Care practice plan.

One of your most important daily practices to begin with is to get back to Restorative Sleep.

One of the most powerful tools to assist? Richard Miller's Yoga Nidra practice that can be found here : www.irest.org

Let Zen Centered be your repetitious daily yoga practice.

Yoga is Medicine, Movement and Radical Self Care

What is Yoga but a union of the body and the mind and the spirit?

Make Lifeforce Yoga a key component of your daily Radical Self Care action plan.

For body mind and spirit to rest and restore

Yogis realized thousands of years ago that changing dysfunctional habits is largely a matter of the mind. It was the mind that was the yogi's most interesting subject of study.

The true intention of their daily yoga practice was to access this "enlightened awareness" through taming the fluctuations of the mind." From Yoga as Medicine by T. McCall, M.D.

Ancient yogis practiced yoga daily to create new habits or what they called "samskaras" Modern scientists call these new neural pathways that can be strengthened with repetitious yoga practice.

Do what ancient yogi masters did.

Let Zen Centered be your repetitious daily yoga practice.

Essential Yoga Principles : Foundation for Daily Radical Self Care Practices

Opening Story : *When I began to focus on one of the essential yoga principles of healthy medicine – "do no harm" I was able to see how I was doing harm in the way I was ignoring my need to heal my own mind as well as my body. I could no longer deny my self.*

Topic 1 : Let go of Pain Belief "No Pain No Gain " to appreciate the value of Patanjali's yogic principle of universal health – "Do No Harm" Hippocrates agreed and so do I.

- ~ Follow the Yoga Prescriptives found in this guide to help you begin a simple morning and evening yoga practice as your next step into Radical Self Care

Topic 2 : Respect Your Body's Resistance as a Signal to Take a Pause : Just Breathe into your Body as Source – your Zen Center

- ~ Learn more about how to "respect the resistance" and "play the yogic edge" to reset your intentions for Absolute Compassion in the way you move your Body!

Topic 3 : Tune in to Explore with Awareness and Breath : Just Be Present to the Rhythm of Breath : listen to the sound of your breath as if it is the ebb and flow of the ocean.

Exercise : Meet your Self on the Mat : Follow "Breath as a Bridge" guided practice below. Integrated body, breath and visualization

1. Meet your Self on the Mat : Choose either Sitting Lotus or Standing Mountain pose

2. <u>Tune in to your Breath :</u> choose alternative nostril breath (see guided practice) and Guided Visualization : Breath as the Bridge between the Body and the Mind

MINDFUL MOVEMENT AS MEDICINE

FOUNDATIONAL YOGA PRACTICES : Essential Yoga

<u>Core Principles of your Zen Centered Daily Practice</u>

1. Safety First : Do No Harm
2. Follow basic precautions and basic protocol!
3. Review any medical physical conditions for contraindications ; some yoga practices are not appropriate for every body because no two bodies are exactly alike!
4. Think of a Zen Centered yoga practice as a discovery process to learn the poses to best fit your individual Intuitive Body
5. If anything you do hurts, don't do it!
6. If a pose is uncomfortable or awkward, come out of the pose and readjust your stance, adjust your posture to ensure you are fully

supported in your foundational pose, breathe to relax and get comfortable; then begin again

7. Always err on the side of caution – the opposite of "no pain no gain"
8. Ease into the pose; avoid fast forced movements!
9. Slow and Steady with a focus on ease and effort ; no straining over stretching or over extending necessary
10. Avoid forcing your self into it to avoid 99% of yoga injuries
11. Avoid perfect poses your mind thinks you should look like ; focus on listening to your breath and body sensations as your guide
12. Avoid acting on competitive urges to be the best with others or to best others
13. Repetition with Restorative yoga Practice to build a bridge and foundation of strength ; then go yoga flow and ease into playing the edge
14. discover the power of playing the yogic edge to find new ways to renew and revitalize the Intuitive Body (see guided practice for step by step instructions on "respect the resistance" and "play safe the yogic edge")

also see : www.Yogajournal.com for more in depth guided practices and additional pose and yoga flow sequences.

Find your Zen Center : this is a specially designated time in your Zen Zone to do your yoga practice with lavender mist and music for sound healing

The Power of Mindful Movement : Yoga Pose

In our daily ZC yoga practice, we set our intentions on the following:

1. feel the pose come to life
2. sense the response of the breath
3. sense the sensations in movements of stretch release and relax

4. sense where the yogic edge is to build strength and flexibility before more endurance

Zen Centered Foundational Practices : Essential Daily Yoga

* Refer to section "Essential Yoga Guided Practice" for step by step guide

Essential Restorative Yoga Pose Practices

This section will help you identify WHAT yoga practices to do as part of your Radical Self Care Daily Plan of Action. The following section "Essential Yoga Guided Practice" offers you a step by step guide to each pose.

1. Sitting lotus pose : fully supported spine
2. Standing mountain pose : fully aligned in precision
3. Reclining savasana : fully restorative

Essential Yoga Breath Practices

To begin with simple intentional breath practices, focus on the following:

1. Breath is the Bridge Between the Body and the Mind
2. SKY Breath Practice Sequences
3. Integrated Breath & Sound : Just Say Ommmmmmm

Essential Mindfulness Meditations

1. Serene scene

2. Mindfulness circuit training
3. Sky Mountains/Sky Lakes
4. Circle of Light

ZC Mindful Practice : Body Scan Healing with Sensate Focus

1. Body Scan
2. Sensate Focus
3. Defusing Sensation
4. Grounding in center

Essential Yoga Flow Sequences

1. Sun Salutations : energizing flow
2. Moon Salutations : relaxing flow
3. Yoga Nidra : restorative rest flow
   - see www.irest.org for guided practice

Essential Breath : Take Ten to Tune In :

1. Ten second breath practice
2. put a pause in it
3. listen to its beat
4. press your fingertips to your wrist to feel the heart beat

ALIGN

Zen Centered : The Source : The Five Sensible Senses

Chapter : The Power of the Five Senses : Tapping into your Five Senses

Personal Narrative : *"When I was burnt out, I felt so numbed out, I was completely unaware of my five senses. My autopilot was on overdrive. When my friend first gave me an adult coloring book, we both laughed about my "inner child" but later I found myself seriously into coloring in the book. It was no joke how calm and relaxed I felt after spending quiet time with my colored pens and adult coloring books. "*

Tune In to your Five Senses

Access the healing power of five sensory awareness : sight, sound, scent, texture, taste. Get better acquainted with each one of the five to recall its purpose, how does it serve the Intuitive Body? Recall how to access each of the five senses with simple Zen Centered guided imagery practices.

Let ZC help you Get in Touch: Become attuned to the sensations of intuitive body resonance : Focus on feelings of relaxation peace serenity calmness

Topic 1 : by our nature we rely most heavily on our sense of sight.

- ~ Access the Power of your Mind's Eye by Focusing your gaze on a fixed point. This triggers the part of the brain that is called the Reticular Activating System and is a state of expansive awareness.
- ~ have you ever felt a sense of "awe" or fascination? A sense of curiosity and inquisitiveness/? This is the Reticular Activator System in the Brain. It is the portal to the creative resourceful brain that automatically seeks to not only survive but thrive in optimal intelligence.

Topic 2 : by our nature we rely most heavily on our sense of sight.

- ~ Some estimates suggest that we take in 70% of our sensory information through the eyes, leaving only 30% for the remaining four senses.
- ~ Colors patterns and shapes all lend themselves to a banquet of visual sensations, a feast for the eyes, Familiar images bring comfort. New images can inspire and exhilarate.
- ~ Focused attention can enhance our capacity to be our best. Mental imagery and guided visualization have long been known to create a sense of calm and inner peace.
- ~ They are known for restoring a sense of Wholeness and as a powerful way to heal grief trauma and everyday stress reactions!

Guided Imageries : Enhancing your Meditation Practice with Visualizations

These guided practices can be done inside or out; be certain to find a quiet resting place where you can sit comfortably with your spine fully supported. Take a few moments to settle in comfortably and focus your attention on the rhythm of your breath.

ZC Guided Practice : Mirrored stillness. Should you happen to come across a small pond in the early morning before the sun kicks up the winds, you may notice something special. Naturalists call it "mirrored stillness" water so calm it reflects the trees the sky and the clouds and all that is around the shores. When we look at a still body of water, the image of calm settles into our unconscious mind and promotes a deep sense of relaxation throughout the body and mind.

ZC Intention: Visit a pond and take a picture of the image and place it in your Zen Center meditation center.

ZC Guided Practice : Rest your Attention on a Visual Cue to Visualize

Choose : A candle Flame : light a candle. Let your eyes rest on the blue center of the flame as you focus all your attention on the dancing blue flame. Breathe quietly and notice how your body begins to relax into the surface where you are sitting. Listen to the sound of your breath.

Next expand your attention to outside the blue flame and rest all of your attention on the dancing orange flame. Rest in this awareness, breathing slowly smoothly and deeply as you allow all of your attention to be absorbed by the dancing yellow flame.

Next allow your attention to hold the whole of the flame, dancing and shifting in blue and orange light.

Exercise : Zen Centered Guided Imagery : Visualize : Beyond the Meadow

In a comfortably, fully supported resting position, close your eyes and focus your attention on your breath.

Next let your attention rest on the image of a grassy meadow high in the mountain summit.

Allow your imagination to work for you.

Notice how the meadow of lavender and sunshine is embraced by the mountain majestic. Breathe deeply while you contemplate her beauty and feel the warmth of sunshine against the coolness of your skin.

As you contemplate the wonder, Does the blue sky touch the purple mountain peaks or do the purple mountain peaks reach up to touch the sky? Breathe deeply and fully embrace the sensations of calm serene beauty.

Stand tall and anchor your feet to the ground.

Exercise : Zen Centered Guided Imagery : Sky Lakes
Sit quietly in a comfortably supported resting position as you settle into the rhythm of your breath. Recall the beauty of the sky lakes resting peacefully beneath the limitless blue skies. Deep reflective pools hidden in the highest peaks of the Himalayan mountains, tranquil pools of reflective stillness.

All is calm.

All is bright, reflected in the soft shadows of light dancing on the water.

All is right.

here in the now.

Bteathe deeply and notice how cools the breeze feels on your skin and the smell of pine and earth and sweet floral essence.

Notice where in your body you let go of tension and soften into the pleasant sensations of warm energy filling up this space.

as you rest on the surface of the tranquil blue sky lake, listen in to the sounds of stillness and the whispering of the breath within your body, like wind whispering in the leaves of the trees.

The Power of Color to Heal the Intuitive Body

Colors have a powerful impact on our emotions and therefore our moods Because different wavelengths of light manifest as various colors, you will find that you are drawn to particular colors that relate ot the areas of the body or psyche that require critical healing attention.

Topic : Color Symbolism :
Red : red is warming and energizing. Red can enhance motivation, joy, vitality and passion. Connected with the root chakra, red stimulates the survival instinct and counters low energy.

Orange: Traditionally a hue associated with love and fertility. Orange inspires upbeat, happy emotions. It is linked with the sacral chakra and used to stimulate creativity, positivity and sexual energy.

Yellow : strengthens memory and intellect and fosters cheerfulness. Yellow is linked with the solar plexus chakra and is used to boost the digestive system, pancreas and adrenal glands. The adrenals are especially impacted by cortisol, a stress related hormone associated with high levels of burn out.

Green : associated with growth, spring and youth as well as renewal. Green has calming harmonizing qualities and is very powerful in relieving anxiety and stress. It links with the heart chakra and is used to balance the immune system, lungs and heart. Green also helps deal with issues of love and self esteem .

Blue : Cooling and soothing, blue inspires tranquility and calmness. . It is symbolic for infinity, devotion, faith and chastity. Linked with the throat chakra, blue is used to ease throat ailments and unblock problems with communication.

Indigo : A spiritually uplifting hue, indigo helps calm the mind and promotes restful sleep. Indigo is associated with the third eye and promotes inspiration

<u>Violet</u> : This color fosters spiritual refinement and insight. Linked with the crown chakra, it stimulates the pituitary gland, Hormones and growth.

*For more on Chakras : <u>The Chakra Secret</u> by Michelle Hastie Thompson
https://www.goodreads.com/en/book/show/25329361-the-chakra-secret

Healing with Meditations and Mandalas :

<u>Personal Narrative</u> : *during my prolonged period of recovery, I found contemplating the colors and shapes of the mandala instead of the ceiling and found it to be surprisingly calming and soothing for my overly busy mind.*

A mandala is a symbolic picture or pattern used in meditation. Its various motifs its colors and geometry are specifically designed to bring about inner focus and inner peace. Mandalas most often take the form of a circle – a shape that represents the self, the Earth, the sun, the cosmos and the state of wholeness that is healing.

When we rest our gaze upon a mandala, the mind becomes as still as the surface of a pool of water. From the profound depths of tranquility emerges insight and our innate healing powers.

"by taking this path, we move toward…a realization of our true nature – which, like the circle of the mandala, is boundless and perfect. Experiencing such a deep sense of unity is immensely healing " (by Lisa Tenzin Dolman from <u>Healing Mandalas)</u>

Because healing begins at a deeply profound level and is not something we can consciously control, setting aside time for mandala meditation creates space for healing and wholeness.

Carl Jung asserted that mandalas are a key to personal transformation because they represent "an archetype of wholeness" Contemplating a mandala allows us to expand beyond our limited perspectives and reveal the interconnectedness of all beings in the universe. Not only does this help us feel more complete, but it gives us a glimpse into our spiritual nature.

Mandala meditations help us feel more whole by strengthening our connection with our essential nature. This is especially relevant in an overly saturated culture of technology and gadgets and is an extremely accessible way to begin- or enhance -- a meditation practice.

Ancient Traditions :

Humans have created mandala like designed since the earliest of times across tradition and cultures. Our distant ancestors left marks on the walls of caves and traced patterns in the sand or placed stones in sacred alignments like those at Stonehenge. In Indian, Tibetan and Chinese cultures, mandalas have always been viewed as a path to enlightenment.

The Science of Mandalas : Mandalas and the Mind

The symmetries repetitions and contrasts of mandala patterns create a hypnotic effect on the mind and causes changes in the rhythms of your brainwaves. As in all forms of meditation, the mandala safely settles the mind into first an Alpha, then a Theta state of mind – which has proven benefits for the mind and the body.

Beta brainwaves : correspond with the state of alertness and concentration

Alpha brainwaves : associated with a state of relaxation. In this state of mind your ability to visualize and be creative is enhanced.

Theta Brainwaves : This state of mind nourished intuition and memory. It encourages insight and deep healing

Delta Brainwaves: correlate with a state of deep sleep

Chapter : Healing with the Sense of Smell :

it is said that the sense of smell is the least used of all five senses, Yet it is one the most powerful senses we have. This is because the olfactory nerves are linked to both memory and emotion – which are stored in the Body unless we process the feelings about our life experiences.

Science has proven negative and positive emotions alter the complex chemistry of the body, and these changes cause an over-production of cortisol and adrenalin.

Research also shows that aromatherapy is an effective boost to the stress depleted immune system, especially in cases of post traumatic stress and depression. Regular treatments of aromatherapy massage can break the cycle of an over-activated Sympathetic Nervous System while boosting the integrity of the immune system.

Aromatherapy is the art and science of using the essential oils produced by plants and are found in the aromatic flowers, leaves, fruits, woods, barks and roots.

Healing with Aromatherapies :

"There are fifty million smell receptors located at the top of the nasal cavity, the size of a postage stamp." (www.quiessence.com)

Aromatherapies work to lift depression and better a troubled state of mind by stimulating the neurotransmitter, serotonin. is naturally produced by the body to keep moods balanced and revitalize the Parasympathetic Nervous System. essential oils blended with lavender, sweet marjoram, clary sage, sandalwood, frankincense and ylang ylang can be used to soothe irritability and balance a depressed mood.

Essential oils are the fragrant, highly concentrated found naturally in various parts of a plant. They are what give the plant its characteristic aroma and contain the healing power of the plant from which it was extracted.

Essential oils are located in tiny secretory structures found in various parts of the plant – like lea (eucalyptus), berries (juniper), grasses (palmarosa), flowering tops (lavender), petals (rose), roots (angelica), zest of fruit (orange), resins (frankincense) and wood (cedar).

A typical essential oil contains more than 100 different chemical compounds, each of which exhibits a specific therapeutic property. When the Floral essences are blended with essential oils, they are highly therapeutic for balancing the mood, calming the body and quieting the mind. Virtually all essential oils possess antiseptic properties, but many also have antifungal, antiviral and antibacterial, anti-depressant and anti-anxiety properties.

Ancient civilizations in China, Egypt, India and the Middle East have used aromatic oils as medicines for the body and mind.

"The Chinese 'Yellow Emperor's Classic of Internal Medicine', was written in 2697 BC and is the oldest surviving medical book in China. This landmark text contains information about the properties of over 300 different plants and their medical uses" www.quinessence.com/history-of-aromatherapy

Ancient Medicines : Hippocrates studied and documented over 200 different herbs he used in body mind therapies like baths and massage. He also prescribed the use of herbs like valerian and hypericum. Hippocrates was one of the first physicians to treat the whole body as one with holistic medicines like food, plants and movement.

The Science of Essential Oils as Medicine

From the European Journal of Preventive Cardiology, a study done in 2012 found …" essential oils commonly used to treat stress, such as bergamot, lowered heart rate and blood pressure following short-term exposure. In addition to reducing the risk of cardiovascular disease, this has positive effects on the symptoms of anxiety." www.quinessence.com

Other research has shown how essential oils combined with massage and music dramatically reduced the stress. A study done in the Journal of Clinical Nursing found that aromatherapy massages given to nurses dramatically reduced their anxiety!

In 2011, a study at the National Center for Biotechnology Information showed bergamot worked to reduce hormone responses to stress and has a balancing effect on the nervous system.

Appealing to your Senses : The use of aromatic essential oils appeals to both the sense of smell AND your sense of touch. Because the skin organ for the human sense of touch is the skin, it is the largest sense organ – and unlike others – is not located at any specific place, but the entire body. Our sense of touch uses many different receptors that helps us respond to different stimuli – including pain, pressure, tension, temperature, texture, shape, weight, contours and vibrations.

Therapeutic Touch

Touch is fundamental to health and well-being. The loving touch of another can transform our experience of pain and create a deep sense of calm in a loving bond. Caressing the fur of a pet animal is a simple yet powerful way of calming and connecting.

It is also true we can gently touch our own skin, massage our temples, gently tap on pressure points to release and relax. When your skin is stimulated by loving touch or massage, it releases many healing chemicals that enhance immune function, improve circulation, and promote restful sleep.

You can give yourself the healing benefits of touch every day with an Ayurvedic self-massage or abhyanga.

If you are feeling excessively stressed and ungrounded, use heavy, warm oils such as sesame or almond. If you are feeling irritated or overheated, try cooling oils such as coconut, sunflower or olive.

Radical Self Care for Burn Out :

We already know that a prolonged period of physical illness can be a catalyst for a negative mind and mood AND weaken the immune system. Because a weakened immune system will be more vulnerable to further dis-ease, dis-stress or infection, aromatherapy can be a powerful remedy in reversing the cycle of psycho-somatic distress.

Aromatherapy is a powerful form of medicine to both treat and prevent stress related illness. When used properly, there are no negative side effects – unlike many pharmaceutical medications commonly prescribed.

Which essential oils help with anxiety?

Some of the best essentials oils for treating anxiety are bergamot, lavender, frankincense, sweet orange and patchouli.

Nervine refers to essential oils that strengthen the nervous system like : geranium, basil, peppermint, vetiver, marjoram

Sedatives refer to essential oils that soothe and calm the nervous system like : bergamot, cedarwood, frankincense, neroli, mandarin, orange

Best essential oils for depression :

lemongrass, patchouli, peppermint, rosemary, sage, sandalwood, thyme, ylang ylang

Healing Botanical Prescriptives :

<u>Lavendar</u> calms stormy emotions like panic, insomnia and depression; aids in sleep and is beneficial to the skin.

<u>Myrrh</u> has a cooling effect on heated emotions

<u>Nutmeg</u> dispels anxiety relieves aches and pains.

<u>Orange</u> aids in relaxation calms hyperactivity Studies have shown that sweet orange essential oil improves mood and decreases cortisol levels. To use : Add four to five drops of sweet orange essential oil to 10ml of carrier oil and massage into the back of the neck, wrists and the bottom of the feet.

<u>Patchouli</u> is sedative that helps to relax and balance restorative well being. is earthy sweet and musky. It is excellent for dry skin care and is an antidepressant, antiseptic, astringent, aphrodisiac sedative and is use as a tonic to soothe inflammation.

<u>Bergamot</u> is a calming uplifting scent and is used for nervous tension, anxiety, insomnia and depression. The delicate citrus like aroma is used to relieve all types of tension and can be used as a massage oil, in a warm bath or in a mist defusers.

<u>Frankincense i</u>s a sedative essential oil and helps promote deep breathing, relieve high blood pressure and is soothing to the body.

<u>Peppermint </u>is widely used to treat mental fatigue depression and headaches; it also bolsters confident :

<u>Sandalwood</u> lifts mood relaxes body and mind

<u>Sage</u> helps calm nervousness insomnia grief and overexertion

<u>Vanilla</u> calms elevates mood and is a strong aphrodisiac

Cedar relaxes the analytical mind promotes healing dreams and creates inner harmony

Eucalyptus is good for aches pains and muscle stiffness ; clears congestions.

Ylang Ylang helps lower blood pressure and reduces rapid heart rate. It is also used to fight depression and strengthen the nervous system.

Healing Prescriptive : As part of your Daily Practice : Rub on soles of feet, inhale in mist defuser to aid sleep. Use in bath salts to soothe body and relax nervous system. Use lavendar scented essential oils or skin cremes post bathing.

Mindful Practice Exercise : PM Practice to include : restorative yoga, bathing with lavendar and music ; follow by Yoga Nidra for a deep and restful sleep.

Also See Zen Centered : Healing the Intuitive Body with Botanicals coming summer 2020 for an expansive guide on healing with plant medicines made of flower essences and essential oils.

See www.grapeseedcompany.com for Essential Oils blends to use in your Daily Radical Self Care practices.

Chapter : The Power of Sound to Restore and Renew

Sound healing is used to treat symptoms of a number of conditions, including anxiety, post traumatic stress and depression.

Some of the benefits of sound healing include lower stress, lower blood pressure, lower cholesterol level, lower risk for coronary artery disease and stroke. Because the auditory nerve is closely connected with the limbic system, sounds can have a profoundly healing effect on mood, sleep and pain management.

"Music is one of a small set of human cultural universals evoking a wide range of emotions, from exhilaration to relaxation, joy to sadness, fear to comfort, and even combinations of these " https://www.healthline.com/health/sound-healing#how-it-works

Music can be used to intentionally regulate mood in the way Neurosurgeons often use music to enhance concentration and focus, armies to coordinate movements and increase cooperation and athletes to increase motivation and stamina.

Ancient Tradition : The idea that 'music is medicine' has deep roots into human history through the healing rituals practiced in pre-industrial, tribal-based societies.

Healing with sound is believed to date back to ancient Greece, when music was used as a remedy for mental illness. Throughout history, music has been used to boost morale in military troops, help people work faster and more productively, and even ward off evil spirits by chanting. In modern culture, music continues to be used to promote health and well-being inside hospitals, clinical settings and in pain management, relaxation, psychotherapy, and personal growth.

Research on the Biology of Music : When the university of chicago's medicine created a healing arts program for their medical student, they added music and fine arts into the curriculum. Why?

Because science shows us Music has a profound effect on the brain and the body!

- ~ Biorhythms and Biochemistry Shifts : The brain changes are reflected in EEG and EKG measure of heart rates pulse and breathing
- ~ Cortisol levels decrease when listening to calming music
- ~ Music slows the Autonomic Nervous System : Physiologically our bodies tend to sync into the musical beat. This helps activate movement and engage your body's motor functions.

<u>Topic</u> : Trust your intuitive Body naturally responds to sound !

we can verify with science as our heart rate and brain waves shift as well when we notice how music movement in the body rhythms. Body rhythms can help shift biorhythms.

<u>Movement and the Felt Sense</u> : Tune in to Develop Trust with your "Felt Sense." You know how it is, when you don't over think it, it is a feeling you feels when your body just begins to move with the rhythm of the music.

- ~ Music can drown out the noisy and the mindless so you can get into the feeling of your Intuitive Body.
- ~ Music's power to relax is revealed in the subtleties and complexities of melody, pitch, timbre harmony and tone.

<u>Research</u> : In a research study done by Labbe et al in 2007, they found playing classical music ten minutes a day has been shown to calm and quell negative emotions and quiet the physiological arousal associated with the stress response.

Music therapist found the movements of the heart muscle tend to synchronize with the beat of the music. Breathing patterns reflected this shift as well. Certain songs can turn sadness to laughter, frustration to calmness, anger to joy in a matter of minutes.

<u>Music and Movement as Radical Self Care</u> : What if you were to consciously focus on music as a way to heal your depleted body?

- ~ How would it feel to let the music move your choice? Play music to bypass any and all thought resistance. Ease into it. Let the rhythm move your Body.
- ~ Exercise : <u>Choose a theme song</u>, a soundtrack for your day and bedtime lullaby to fall into deep and restful sleep .

Integrated Meditation and Sound : Meditation is one of the primary modalities used in Ayurveda medicine. Sometimes referred to as "The

Science of Life, "Ayurvedic medicine is the comprehensive, natural health care system that originated in the ancient Vedic times of India.

The term "meditation" inclusively refers to contemplation, concentration and the use of nature sounds like the ocean, guided meditation, meditative movement exercises such as Yoga and tai chi, qigong, breathing exercises, and Mantra. All of these techniques work holistically with the senses, mind, intellect, and emotions.

https://www.ncbi.nlm.nih.gov/pmc/articles/PMC4895748/

*Zen Centered Radical Self Care incorporates both sound and mantra into the Meditations you practice in your Three Point Yoga Prescriptives.

Another kind of Sound healing is called "binaural beats" which stimulates the brain into a specific state using pulsing sounds. This rhythmic pulsing encourages your brain waves to align to the frequency of the beat. This kind of sound therapy can help induce enhanced focus, entranced state, relaxation, or sleep.

Though more research is needed, there's some evidence-based medicine showing that audible brainwave entrainment reduces anxiety, pain, symptoms of premenstrual syndrome and improves behavioral problems in children.

Listen in to Dr. Andrew Weil's : Vibrational Sound Healing here https://www.soundstrue.com/store/vibrational-sound-healing-593.html

The Power of Meditation and Mantra

If we look to ancient medicine, all traditions of the world have used sound for healing, whether it is the beating of a drum, a tambourine, a bell, a gong, or a sacred chant. Through ancient Vedic Tradition of India the use of sound has been refined over thousands of years to formulate it into what is now called "Vedic Science of Mantras."

Mantras are specific sounds or vibrations when either chanted aloud or repeated silently heal, transform and awaken.

All Zen Centered Three Point Yoga Prescriptives include some kind of Mantras for you to explore and experience as you begin your Radical Self Care Daily Practices.

Healing With Sound : Move with your Intuitive Body

Mindful Exercise : Nature Sounds : What are the Sounds of Nature that soothe you when you are feeling down? What are the Sounds of Nature that calm you when you feel irritated and edgy? Be Present to How Nature Sounds can change how you think and how you feel.

Mindful Exploration Exercise : Choose to listen to Singing Bowls and Wind Chimes and write a mindful journal review about your observations

Mindful journal Inquiry : Ask : How do I feel physically mentally and emotionally before and after I meditate on the feeling in my body?

Plants as Medicine : Holistic Healing with Plants

Return to Nature's Pharmacy

herbal medicines are a catalyst of natural healing, so we encourage you to make room in your life to review the value of Plant Medicines.

"Nature is the healer of disease" Hippocrates

Natural Herbal remedies :

did you know that over 1/3 of prescribed synthetic drugs are obtained from plants? Herbal remedies work through active biochemical compounds and often the whole herb may be more effective than isolated pharmaceutical compounds. It is true the whole of a plant's active substances is greater than the sum of its individual constituents.

Since herbal medicines can be a catalyst for natural healing, we support Nature's wisdom in radical self care practices that incorporate the use of Food as Medicine and Herbs as holistic remedies.

We also support the use of Nutraceuticals.

What's a nutraceutical?

A nutraceutical is a special class of supplements. Nutraceuticals, herbs and nutrients can be used as first line treatments for mild to moderate depressions with complementary alternative medicines (sometimes called CAMs)

These are some examples :* SAM-e, Rhodiola Rosea, st. john's wort depression and for anxiety kava, valerian, lemon balm, passionflower and chamomille.

St. John's Wort was a little known herb until it came to attention as a natural alternative to anti-depressant medthe safety and lack of addiction potential still make St. John's Wort a good alternative to prescription drugs.

Chamomile is a herbal remedy that relieves the discomfort of muscle cramps, eases digestive problems including gastro-intestinal irritation, ulcers, colitis and irritable bowel syndrome, plus it reduces anxiety. Used as an herbal tea it also works as a remedy for insomnia.

Ginseng is an herbal remedy called an adaptogen, a substance that can ward off physical and mental strain so the body can return to normal levels of functioning. Ginseng was/is often used in Chinese medicine and is also recommended by herbalists for fatigue and stress. Ginseng s especially effective as a tea to be used when recovering from an illness.

*Recommended Resource: For more guidance see, <u>Healing with Yoga Nutrition and Herbs</u> by P. Gerbarg et al. .

Plants as Food Medicines : Fuel your Nutrition :

"let food by thy medicine and medicine by thy food" Hippocrates

Ayurvedic medicine categorizes food into six tastes: sweet, sour, salty, pungent, bitter, and astringent. Each of the tastes has a unique effect on our mind-body physiology and provides the flavor that makes eating a pleasure. If you include the six tastes in a meal, you will get the nutrients you need and will feel completely satisfied.

If you are suffering from burn out, you are most likely suffering from nutritional deficiencies that can be easily corrected with simple healthy whole food choices that include high complex carbohydrates, whole plants foods, essential fat and healthy proteins.

Becoming tuned into the Body also means becoming more aware of how you are gathering and preparing your foods as well as how you are celebrating the lost art of mealtime and the pleasure of dining.

Eating foods that nourish your body and spirit is an essential part of a healthy way of life which is what the word "diet" originally meant. Health in this context has to do with living in harmony with your body's natural needs and in balance with other humans and the planet. Radical self care means making Healthy Eating a high priority so food can be a healing medicine for your body.

When you practice Mindful Eating, you are not counting calories or carbs or calculating what food you will or will not put in your body. Mindful eating is learning how to be Present and tuned in the experience of hunger, fullness and satisfaction. Mindful eating is an experience in being fully present and tasting the texture the flavor and savoring the scent.

Becoming more present helps you discover the body's hunger for healthy fuel for the body is not the same as emotional eating out of a deep sense of fatigue and exhaustion or a chronic problem with dieting or unhealthy weight loss habits. This awareness can be soothing in and of itself.

Mindful practice will help you move forward from here. What would we learn if we turn to ancient tradition?

Ancient Traditions

Thousands of years ago, people in the Far East realized that not only body structure but even human nature can be changed by attending to the manner in which we drink and eat. For these ancients eating and drinking were considered the most important rituals in the divine art of life. Among other cultures, culinary art is also an art of life.

The Sufis for instance, hold that our health, happiness, liberty and judgment are all affected by what happens in our kitchens. We know many medical conditions can be dramatically improved or even cured with correction of diet and lifestyle. Once you incorporate healing practices into your life it is easy for your body to rebuild itself through what you eat and how it is prepared.

In Chinese medicine a doctor's role is to help patients learn how to take care of themselves. The physician is also thought of as a gardener. The human body is considered a garden where each species is connected to every other. The physicians task is to tend the garden the way you tend roses – to cultivate and nourish and teach the patient to be gardeners too .

When the doctor helps them understand how to summon the healing faculties of their own bodies for recovery, the doctor is encouraging the patient to listen to her body.

Knowingness.

Nature embodies mysteries that modern technology cannot fathom. The wisest choice we can make is to educate ourselves regarding the Radical Self Care of own bodies and to look to the simplicity of Nature as our essential guide.

Mindfulness of the Intuitive Body : The Sense of Taste :

Engage with your five sensory awarenesses to enhance your dining experience. Begin to appeal to your scent of smell taste and texture by becoming more aware of your own relationship with food, emotion and eating.

This means being mindfully present to the toxic food substances you may be putting in your body on a daily basis that diminishes the health of the Intuitive Body. There is a rich array of phytonutrients in various foods we can focus on in place of useless carb or calorie counting. Food synergy is a way we can focus on the interaction of two or more nutrients and other healthful substances in food to see how they work together. to achieve an effect that each individually is unable to match.

The body benefits immeasurably from a constant rich infusion of Super Foods – whole foods filled with phytonutrients as well as all macro and other micronutrients. Appealing to your sense of taste and the thousands of taste buds on your tongue is another exercise in mindfulness to help you become present, aware and relaxed. Just like mindful eating is the key to shifting appetite and eating habits in a positive direction, slowing down to reflect on your eating habits is worth the time it takes to go from sickness into health,

Healing through the Sense of Taste : Scientific studies of the tongue show that the number of taste buds can greatly vary from individual to individual which is why some people are most "taste sensitive" to foods than others due to the 1000s of taste buds.

The Healing Power of Herbs and Spices :

Historically herbs and spices have been used to enhance flavors and provide unique taste to foods. The very same spices come from plants whose traditional uses have included medicinal purposes to prevent and heal disease.

Spices can work together synergistically to provide nutraceutical benefits to the Intuitive Body. Choosing to use herbs and spices to enhance a whole food based diet is a powerful way to the replace foods products that are overly refined, highly processed, refined sugars, trans-fat, salts, preservatives or other toxic chemicals.

do you know there are over 25,000 phytochemicals, living plant compounds found in whole plant foods? Phytochemicals are the superfood food compounds we want to include in our daily food as medicine plan!

Mindful planning would include spices like these – not only because they are natural flavor enhancers but because they have medicinal benefits to the body/mind : Such as:

- Cinnamon lowers blood sugar and stimulates circulation,
- nutmeg relieves nausea;
- cloves are anti inflammatory;
- ginger relieves nausea, gastrointestinal distress or morning sickness
- peppermint inhibits the growth of bacteria;
- cumin helps with digestion, cayenne pepper increased metabolism;
- chili powder eases pain;
- curry powder safeguards your brain;
- cardamom soothes indigestion.

<u>Mindful Nutrition</u> : A Zen Centered Radical Self Care practices ALWAYS includes mindful eating.

A focus on positive mood food choices like : pumpkin seeds, chia seeds, kombucha, salmon, quinoa, chickpeas, kale, watercress, blueberries and Greek yogurt are some examples.

Cinnamon, garlic, ginger, peppermint are some examples of plants that can be used to season foods to avoid use of artificial seasonings and overly processed foods.

*For more specific food, recipe and menu choices, see <u>The Mindfully Mediterranean Un-Diet Plan </u> and recipe guides. This simple guide is offers Five Essential Principles and Practices and is based on the Mediterranean Food Pyramid.

ACTIVATE

YOGA PRESCRIPTIVES

<u>Chapter : Essential Practices for Your Radical Self Care Dailies</u>

Opening Story : I discovered that I found my own "yoga rhythm" by going through the steps of Meeting my Self on the Mat. Even if I got to the mat and expressed all my "I don't feel like it" in body motion instead of sedentary immobility.

Topic 1 : Dailies are your Daily Dedications : Show Respect for your Intuitive Body

Topic 2 : Practice the yoga Principle of "sankalpa" to activate your practice by setting a daily intention.at

Topic 3 : Balance Effort With Ease :the Restive with the Active The healthy body naturally inhabits a space of both SNS – activated and PNS – restorative. Stressed out or burnt out is often fed by "either or" extremes ; to reverse the pattern of go go go, go to a Place to restore –create a Zen Zone By setting aside a ritual to create a safe space to go to, you increase your chances of success in making yoga a daily practice habit.

Exercise : Create your Zen Zone : Gadget Free Zone : Free from Distractions Quiet and Dedicated for Radical Self Care Dailies.

Your Zen Zone could include : mat, Mexican blankets cos they are best for rolling up or folding in squares or using as a blanket to keep you warm during your resting poses. Towel for the same. Pillows to act as bolsters. Yoga blocks yoga balls and a basket to keep them in. candles. Chimes or sounding bowls. Sounds of music or nature Essential oils and/or aromatherapy mists

Chapter : Essential Daily Practices :

Topic 1 : Just Breathe : Take 10 : 10 seconds to 10 minutes

Topic 2 : Meet your Self on the Mat in the Morning : Hand on your Heart and Rest Gentle on Your Belly

Topic 3 : Meet your Self on the Mat in the Evening : Defuse with a Dance Off Then Recline into a Restorative Resting Pose

Exercise : Mindful Exploration and Journal to Track Awareness : Set your Intention to do One Practice a Day of Topic 1 plus either topic 2 or topic 3.

Chapter : The Power of Three : Integrated Intuitive Body Practices to Activate Healing Response

Opening Story : *The more I practiced the 3 point yoga prescriptives, the more I noticed I was relaxing and sleeping better...especially with the yoga nidra guided audio I discovered on Sounds True.*

Topic 1: Three Point Yoga Prescriptive to Rest:

- Yoga moves: upward dog, crocodile, corpse/resting
- Five Sensory Awareness : Nature Sounds of water or other calming soothing sounds
- Herbal Remedies : Botanical Mists or Essential Oils scented with Lavender or

Topic 2 : Three Point Yoga Prescriptive to Restore

- Yoga Moves : restorative yoga practices include legs up the wall and resting corpse
- Mindfulness Mind : use SKY guided visualizations to give your mind new practice with visualization (five sensory sense : visual)
- Healing Sounds and Scents : Choose an Intuitive Body theme music track to record on your smartphone

Topic 3 : Three Point Yoga Prescriptive to Revitalize

- Mindful Body : Fuel your Body with Superfoods : Boost your Fuel Sources
- Mindful Eating Review : What Plant Foods are Missing? Add Super Foods to Boost your Energy*

*see Mindfully Mediterranean Food Guide for superfoods and superfood daily eating plans

Mindful Intentions : Track toxic foods to eliminate and healthy food substitutions one day at a time this week : Use your Journal as a Mindfulness track to Observe Discover and Recover Insight to Add into Plan

Zen Centered Daily Wellness Practice :

Begin in the Now to connect with your Intuitive Body there is no time like the present!

ZC Radical Self Care : Seven Days to Start : Three Point Practice

1. Movement
2. Meditation
3. Essential nutrition
   - detoxify your eating habits
   - purify with essential hydration and whole plant based foods
   - use plants as medicine like herbs for mood balancing and nutraceuticals if needed

Yoga Prescriptive for Healing Intuitive Body : Anxious Mood

If your Pain Body cues are :

Mind/mood: I'm feeling…distracted, spacey, anxious, fearful, worried

Body : indigestion, gas, constipation

Body parts in pain : colon low spine hips thighs bones

Best Zen Centered Practices :

Best asanas : seated, hip openers, seated/lying twists, supported backbends, standing balances, deep squats, warming inversions.

Sounds : Humming breath and breath practices focus on deepening exhalation

Oils : Warming, nourishing, toning, gentle : Essential oil is almond or sesame and botanicals are lavendar and rose

Affirmations : I am safe. My mind is clear and focused.

Meditation : guided meditations ; candle

Body Check in After Practice : you will notice you feel warm, stable, calm with less tension in your lower abdomen. Your mind is peaceful and you feel grounded in calm strength.

Essential Balancing Self Care

1. Keep warm
2. Keep calm
3. Avoid cold, raw foods and drinks
4. Avoid temperature extremes
5. Eat warm foods with spices
6. Add the tastes of salty, sour and sweet
7. Keep a regular routine

Yoga Prescriptive for Agitated Mixed Mood

Mind mood : aggressive, intense, angry, resentful, impatient, critical

Mindful inquiry : what do I want?

ZC IB focus : calm emotions, cool the mind using color and visualization

Pain Body cues: ready for fight ; tense muscles : excessive stomach acidity

Pain Body Scan : small intestine, stomach, liver, gallbladder, spleen

Essential ZC Yoga Practices :

Calming quieting cooling. Relax and avoid overheating

- choose from Asanas : seated wide legged, seated/lying and standing twists, cooling inversions and gentle backbends.
- Focus on deep exhale and holds

Integrated Practices : Sounds : Exhale aaahhhhhhh and Haaaaaa

Essential Oils : Cooling cleansing soothing light : base : coconut, sunflower with botanicals of sandalwood and jasmine

Daily Affirmations : I am one with the universe. I am one. I am.

Pranayamas : begin with even inhale exhale; then move to focus on exhale; cooling breathing

Meditation : Yoga nidra ; loving kindness

Balancing Practices :

- ⁓ Avoid excessive heat
- ⁓ Avoid excessive salt
- ⁓ Add tastes that are bitter sweet and astringent
- ⁓ Avoid spicy foods
- ⁓ Practice yoga during cool time of the day

Best yoga practices to avert natural tendency toward hyper perfectionistic tendencies of heating energizing and forceful breathing, always incorporate cooling poses! Focus on relaxation and surrender

- ⁓ Because of tendencies to be overly goal oriented and competitive, focus on calming and sedating and cooling inverted poses (like forward bends with twists)
- ⁓ Balance outer sensations with inner work by closing eyes and at intervals throughout practice session
- ⁓ Stabilize shoulders and pelvic girdles
- ⁓ Focus on exhalations
- ⁓ Heart chakra for compassion and 6th 7th for intuition insight

After your practice you will feel cool, content, calm and relaxed in your mid abdomen. Your mind is clear and serene, you are emotionally at peace

Yoga Prescriptive for Heavy Lethargic Depression

<u>Pain Body</u> : stubbornly stuck; passive aggressive, depressed, prone to overeating

<u>Physical sites :</u> Lungs feel congested and heart is heavy

<u>Best Yoga Practice</u> : stimulating, warming and challenging

<u>Types of Asanas</u> : standing inverted twists, flowing movements interspersed with holds. Sun or moon salutations, arm balances and all inversions

<u>Sounds</u> : Aummmm Rammmmm

<u>Essential Oils</u> : Warming cleansing stimulating and deep : base is sesame or olive and the botanicals are orange, patchouli and rosemary

<u>Pranayama</u> : Ujjayi, hara

<u>Meditation:</u> Moving meditations with color and visualizations

<u>Best Balancing Practices :</u>

- ~ Lots of exercise and physical activity
- ~ Avoid heavy foods
- ~ Avoid dairy
- ~ Add tastes that are pungent, bitter and astringent
- ~ Vary routine

<u>Best Zen Centered Yoga</u> : Focus on yoga practices that are grounding and create a pleasant consistent repetition. Use a step by step approach

- ~ standing pose like hero to create heat and vitality while opening chest
- ~ backbends that build heat and energy
- ~ breath practices that focus on inhalation and warming pranayamas
- ~ Lion pose to reduce lethargy

- ~ Sun salutations to build heat gradually
- ~ Chakra yoga for balancing

After Practice you will feel warm, invigorated and energized. Your chest and lungs feel open, you heart not heavy but light. Your mind is clear and your senses are vivid and sharp

MINDFUL MIND MEDITATIVE PRACTICES

How do we see the world in new perspectives? Close your eyes to see from another point of view….

Mindful Mind Meditative Practices

The Power of Observing with Presence: Up Close at a Distance

1. Picture a picture in your mind's eye
2. Picture the picture up close; then picture the picture far away
3. Notice how What you Focus on Expands
4. Shift the focus from up close to at a distance ; inside the picture and out

Exercise : Zen Centered Guided Imagery Practice :

Meadows of Lavendar and Sunshine

1. in the meadows of my mind : I find peace and tranquility here..in the present…in the now.
2. what are the scents of the meadow in the morning fresh dew ? how are they different than later when the afternoon sun blankets the meadow in golden warm sunshine? Is the breeze cool or warm on your skin?

Exercise : Zen Centered Guided Imagery and Intentional Breath Practice

Bhramari or Bee Breath

Sit quietly in a relaxed and fully supported position. Close your eyes and relax into the rhythm of your breath.

recall the sound of bees humming in the meadow of deep purple lavendar and golden bright sunshine.

Notice how You are safe here to listen to the beauty of mother nature in sync with the earth.

Breathe deeply into the sound of the bees buzzing in the hive as the queen spins the honeycomb with sweet gold nectar. Notice how pleasant the sound and begin to hum along...as if the sound begins in the back of your throat and rises up into your mind in a pleasant sensation of hmmmmmmmmm

Exercise : Zen Centered Integrated Practice : Body like Mountain :

Stand in Mountain Pose.

Feel how your pose is like the mountain. You are anchored in majestic strength at one with the earth. your body is anchored in strength. Breathe slowly smoothly and deeply as you rest your hand on your belly center.

Reflect again on the purple mountain majestic.

Does the mountain touch the sky? Or....does the sky touch the mountain. Breathe deeply as you contemplate and compare to contrast...peace and tranquility rests within you.

Raise your arms and extend out to the side in the Warrior pose.

Hold this pose as you feel strength throughout your body inside and out. From head to toe. Feel your feet on the ground and wiggle your toes.

Now raise your arms above your head into a sun salutation and clasp your hands together. Relax your shoulders and back the lengthen of your spine. Breathe deeply and look up towards the sky.

Let your arms drift to your sides and allow your self to quietly rest in this standing pose for another minute or two. Open your eyes and allow your self to return to the present.

Notice how relaxed and alert you feel in calm strength.

ZEN CENTERED ESSENTIAL YOGA : GUIDED PRACTICE

SKY Breath : Guided Practice Exercises

SKY or sudarshan Kriya Yoga is a comprehensive course of integrated breath yoga and meditation practices and one of the most effective ways to heal and restore your Intuitive Body.

Since neural pathways for breathing and emotion are intricately intertwined, SKY breath practices are extremely effective in reducing anxiety, insomnia, depression, fatigue, anger and symptoms of post traumatic stress!

Sudarshan Kriya consists of sets of cyclical breathing (no pause between inhalation and exhalation 0 at three rates (slow, medium and fast)

Five integrated breath practices :

1. Ujjayi or ocean sounding breath :
    -   creates a sound using contraction of larynegeal muscles, permitting fine regulation of the respiratory rate.

2. Bhastrika
   - rapid forceful 30 breaths per minute for short bursts (less than one minute) lead to SNS activation followed by emotional calming with mental alertness)

3. aum chanting "Om" "AUM" or "So Ham"
   - this intentional breath practice uses a simple sound "aum" or "so hum" ; This breath practice is shown to decrease Sympathetic Nervous System hyper - activity and may increase vagal tone

4. Sudarshan Kriya (cyclical breathing at varying rates -no pause between inhalation and exhalation three different rates – slow, medium and fast)
   - Coherent or Resonant Breathing is a modern adaptation of the ancient practice of breathing at approximately five breaths per minute.
   - Coherent breathing induces healthy alpha rhythms in the brain!
   - For guided practice see : https://coherentbreathing.com/

5. Alternative Nostril Breathing :
   - Alternative nostril breathing is used in many yoga traditions and is a key practice of your Zen Centered Radical Self Care daily plan.
   - It is easy to learn and generally has a calming effect within ten minutes.

Guided Breath Practice : alternative nostril breath

With the eyes closed, the second and third fingers rest on the bridge of the nose for support. The remaining fingers are used to gently press the side of the nose, alternately closing one nostril or the other.

The practice starts with a slow exhalation breath and then a slow inhalation through the open nostril, switching sides after each complete breath cycle.

Recommended Practice : Ten to 20 minutes of alternate nostril breathing is recommended twice a day as needed for anxiety : Five to ten minutes of this technique prior to meditation enhances meditative or prayer practices. Using a certain number of counts for each breath phase produces different effects. For example, slowly counting to six during the expiration and four during the inspiration is comfortable and beneficial.

Guided Yoga Practice : Right Nostril Breathing (energizing practice)

Sit in a comfortable position with your spine fully supported, your shoulders relaxed and your attention focused on your breath. Make a fist of your right hand.

Next release the thumb and the third and fourth fingers, keeping the index finger and the middle finger folded toward the palm. Close the left nostril with the fourth finger of the right hand. Breathe in through the right nostril. Close the right nostril with the thumb and exhale through the left nostril. Repeat.

Focus on making the inhale and exhale even. Do ten sets then sit quietly and notice the energy in your body.

If you feel too energized, practice a few rounds of Alternate Nostril Breathing to calm and balance. Gradually increase the practice from 10 sets to 20 if you are struggling with an Atypical Depression and feel lethargic, dull or fatigued.

Guided Yoga Practice : Left Nostril (calming practice)

Sit in a comfortable position with your spine fully supported, your shoulders relaxed and your attention focused on your breath. Make a fist of your left hand. Next release the thumb and the third and fourth fingers, keeping the index finger and the middle finger folded toward the palm.

Close the right nostril with the fourth finger of the left hand. Breathe in through the left nostril. Close the left nostril with the thumb and exhale slowly through the right nostril. Repeat.

Focus on making the inhale and exhale even. Do ten sets then sit quietly and notice the energy in your body.

Guided yoga Practice : Alternate Nostril Breath Practice (balancing practice)

Sit in a comfortable seating position with your spine fully supported, your shoulders relaxed. Breathe normally to clear nasal passage as you rest into your sitting bones and begin to focus on your breath.

To begin, inhale deeply through both nostrils, pause slightly, then exhale sharply through the nostrils – lips are slightly parted.

Inhale through the active nostril slowly and deeply. At the end of the inhalation, close the active nostril, then slowly and completely exhale; then inhale through the passive nostril.

Repeat this cycle of inhaling slowly through the open nostril, switching sides after each complete breath cycle.

ZC Daily Yoga Prescriptive : Take ten minutes a day at first, then increase the practice up to twenty minutes of alternate nostril breath twice a day

Integrated SKY Breath Practices : Ocean Sounding Breath : Ujjayi

To begin inhale through your nostrils with a slight construction of your throat – make like a snoring sound. Maintain the slight snoring sound on the exhalation. Imagine you are actually breathing from the back of your throat.

Think of the sound like a wave gently rolling across a pebbly beach. Breathe slowly, expanding the belly, the ribcage and the upper chest.

As you exhale, draw the abdomen in and up to empty your lungs completely. Let the rhythm of your breath be like a lullaby as you continue to practice ten rounds of this breath.

You can also practice Ocean sounding breath throughout your pose sequences.

Integrated Breath Practice : Stair Step Breath

1. Inhale little sips of breath through the nostrils to the count of four until you've reached full lung capacity, then slowly exhale.
2. Slowly inhale as you take small short exhalations, stepping down the stairs until you've emptied your lungs.
3. Repeat inhaling little sips of breath in to capacity, then pause for a count of four before you exhale little sips of breath out.
4. Repeat with breath retention in each step. End with a final repetition of step #1

SKY Integrated Breath Practices with Sound

1. INTEGRATED BREATH AND SOUND :

Begin with a deep inhalation through your nostrils and as you exhale, begin to make a soft hmmmmm sound in the back of your throat until you feel the resonating vibration throughout your throat.

Next place your thumbs on your inner ear lobe and press gently to close the opening of your ear canal; inhale deeply throat your nostrils; as you begin the xhale breath repeat the humming sound from the back of your throat and close your eyes as you feel the gentle resonance of the vibration through the complete exhalation of your breath.

Pause in the suspended moment between this breath and the beginning of the inhalation cycle .

2. Just say Ommm : universal sound of resonance

3. So Ham : quietly say "so" as you inhale to a breath count of four : Pause : exhale to the sound of "hummm" as you count six to eight beats more.

Holistic Body Mind Therapies

This section focuses on Body Mind therapy tools to support you in healing the Pain Profile you identified earlier. Integrating tools like EFT/Tapping, Progressive Muscle Relaxation (PMR) and Lifeforce Yoga Therapies offers relief from mental physical and emotional suffering.

DAILY RESTORATIVE YOGA : Step by Step Guide to Essential Daily Practice

The following section offers you a guided step by step practice for the foundational poses of your daily practice.

Zen Centered Daily Yoga Restorative Practices:

Savasana Resting Relaxation Pose :

1. Rest horizontally on the floor with your spine elongating and shoulder blades flush against the floor. Palms facing up and legs about 8 inches apart.
2. To discover the natural curves of our spine, observe which parts of your spine touch the floor and which parts of your spine curve up away from the floor.
3. the position of your head is crucial in Savasana. If the chin is elevated relative to your forehead, the position tends to be stimulating. If your chin is even with the forehead or slightly lower, it is easier to relax. Use a pillow or folded blanket if needed to elevate the head accordingly.

<u>Version one</u> : place a small folded blanket under your neck to keep the back and front of your neck evenly extended. Relax into the position and observe sensations of relaxation in your body

<u>Version two</u> : a blanket roll under mid thighs. When you use a support under your thighs, it allows your back to be supported and touch the ground. Notice how your back muscles can relax and release the tightness of supporting your back.

<u>Version three</u> : full pose without props. Allow your spoine to rest fully into the natural configurations of the ground while you let go of the muscles in your entire back body by scanning up and down your back body, noticing where you have any tendency to grip. Keep the direction of your body dropping into the lap of the earth as you keep your mind awake but still.

<u>Guided Practice : Legs up the Wall Relaxation:</u>

When properly supported, you will feel a progressive calmness in each pose. Any restlessness or irritation is a sign to readjust supportive bolsters or blankets beneath back and neck so you can relax fully into the pose.

<u>Version one</u> : Back flat on the ground; buttocks against the wall, legs in a cross legged position. The challenge is to get as comfortable on the floor as ;possible with as much of your back in contact with the ground, expanding from your spine. Keep your feed slightly activity, allowing your legs to fold deeply into the pull of gravity. Rest in this position for 1-2 minutes; then switch the cross of your legs and remain in resting position for another 1-2 minutes.

<u>Version two</u> : Legs straight up the wall : back flat on the ground with full extension of the legs. The challenge in this pose is to find the right distance from the wall so your sacrum is flat on the ground while your legs are straight. Experiment with different distances until your back feels no pull or strain. Release and relax. Rest your arms in "cactus position" above you or palms up alongside your body (as in savasana) Rest in this pose 5 to 15 minutes

Version three : supported by a bolster or folded blanket supporting your upper pelvis to the bottom tips of your shoulder blades. Shoulders themselves touch the floor. The challenge in this version is positioning the bolster so that your chest is open but your sacrum and legs are grounded. Play with the distance of your pelvis from the wall and the position of the bolster. Feeling the support of the bolster, relax the curves of your spine. Rest for two minutes more in this pose, noticing the sensations of relaxing deeply into the earth.

Guided Practice : Childs Pose

1. Start by kneeling with the knees slightly separated and the tops of your feet on the floor. Next release your forehead to the floor as you allow your buttocks to sink to the back of your ankles. Bring your arms back along your body with the palms resting up.

Version one : bolster under your torso, head turned to the side. Supporting your front body with a bolster provides a sense of great comfort and safety. Lifting your torso and head encourages the deep folding of your legs and the falling of your weight back on your pelvis toward your h eels Find the connection to the top of your sacrum, your shoulder blades and your tailbone with your m ind and with our breath.

Version two : Place a thin roll between your lower belly and your upper thighs This prop encourages a deeper release of your lower back muscles, creating a tucking of your tailbone and a gentle roundness of your entire spine.

Version three : full pose, belly resting against your thighs, head resting on the floor. *Allow your hips to drop deeper and deeper, letting go of the tension in your calves, knees, front of our shins, the tops of your thighs and your lower back. Allow your hip flexors to soften into your body to restore their natural length.

*place pillow under the forehead or a rolled blanket at the feet for support and comfort. Remain resting in this pose for up to ten minutes.

Guided Restorative Practice : Crocodile Pose :

1. lie on your belly with your legs a comfortable distance apart. Turn your toes either in or out, whichever is more comfortable for you to relax. Fold your arms and place each hand on the opposite elbow, creating a cradle to rest your head. Rest our head on your forearms and relax.
2. Notice your breath as it flows out and in. as your breath flows out, feel how your breath empties, how the exhalation cleanses and releases tension. Ass your breath flows in, feel how your breath fills you, how the inhalation nourishes you and restores fresh energy. Continue to observe the ebb and flow of your breath, feeling it empty and fill your body.
3. Soften our navel and allow your belly to relax into the flow of your breath
4. Notice as you exhale your belly expands and as your exhale your belly contracts into your spine
5. Let each breath flow smoothly slowly and deeply throughout your body from head to toe

Guided Restorative Practice : Yoga Nidra

"yoga nidra" is an intricate form of guided relaxation paired with visualizations while laying in savasana. It relaxes the body, the mind, the nervous system and the subconscious mind in a safe and systemic fashion. The science shows yoga nidra lowers blood pressure, heart rate and decreases stress hormone levels.

The guided practice : listen to Richard Millers guided Yoga Nidra Practice

INTEGRATED BODY MIND THERAPIES:
INTEGRATED BODY MIND THERAPIES

Progressive Muscle Relaxation techniques have long been used to help pain patients manage and can be a simple tool of awareness to help you heal the Pain Mind Body . Think of a pain scale using the continuum of numbers from 1-10 measuring intensity of sensation, 1 is less pain 10 = most intense pain. The Pain Intensity Scale Number helps your brain process and defuse the sensations with this kind of guided practice.

Simple Guided Practice : Body Scan to Defuse Tension

1. Body scan to notice body parts in pain
2. Intentional deep breathing throughout practice : choose Ocean sounding breath to start with
3. Give body part a name and a PINs # 1-10
4. Give the PINs a size shape and a color
5. Use your hands to either Squeeze the Pain in your Fist or Palm the Pain between your Hands
6. Defuse the PINs sensation to a range between 2-5.

Guided Practice : Palming : sit in a comfortable seated position, with your spine fully supported so you can relax.

1. Begin by rubbing your palms together to create a friction for fifteen to twenty seconds.
2. Then place your palms over your closed eyes. Do not press against your eyes or put any pressure on the eyeball themselves. Instead, press on your brow and on the cheeks outside the bony rims of your eye sockets
3. Continue to keep your chest upright but allow your head to gently tip forward.
4. Tune in to the breath and the feeling of warmth in your hands on your face.
5. Notice any colors of textures of the visual patterns beneath your hands. Allow those visual images to fade to black as the muscles of your face let go.
6. Rest in this position for the next two minutes.

EFT Tapping on meridien points to relieve tension

Healing Body Therapies : EFT Tapping or LFY Palming :

EFT Tapping : tapping pressure points on the body ; start with collarbones .

Visit Nick Ortner @ www.thetappingsolution.com

Chapter : PMR to debrief high anxiety panic or depression

1. Body scan : use PINs scale : 1-10
2. Progressive muscle relaxation tools to defuse sensation

Exercise : Guided Practice Body Scan

1. Turn your Attention Inward : pay attention to sensation
2. Mindful Inquiry : Where does your body carry tightness tension or feel heavy and blocked?
3. Body Scan : Your head your shoulders your gut your back
4. Breath Release : notice the tight heavy block and breathe deeply in through your nostrils at the same time. Pause before you exhale deeply through your nostrils. Your lips are slightly parted.
5. Body Center : focus on the flow of your breath into your heart into your belly and rest your hand gently on your belly.

BLENDING ART AND SCIENCE :

"mastery is a blend of science and art." Patanjali

In Natural History's Gold Age, Art and Science were intricately interwoven through the disciplines of illustration and classification. Art inspired crucial advances in science that would not have been possible if not for art. Charles Darwin's adventures were art inspired so were those of Leonardo Di Vinci and Michelangelo?

What do we learn from Art? How to reclassify information into imagery that creates greater meaning. Flexible frameworks; creative expressions uncover inspirations and insights or creative intelligence. A-ha's or moments of inspiration

When we choose to illustrate beauty found in Nature, this becomes an intentional Act of Radical Self Care that will heal your emotional body. In our technology oriented modern cultures, it is too easy to get lost and distracted in our artificial intelligence. When we choose instead an act of creative self expression.

Because creative expression is an expression of the Intuitive Body, we use Creative Journals to access creative intelligence and the way artistic expression can heal and restore. Creative expression renews our human connection with our True Self, other human beings and our true Source – Mother Nature.

Personal Narrative_: I've always kept a journal since I was a young child. We used to call them "diaries" But during time of personal tragedy, loss or other emotional crises, I write more draw more and paint more than I usually would. I am certain without art I would not have made it through the terrible depression I suffered after a series of devastating losses in the middle of my life. In all truth, art saved my life. Art can save your life too.

find your Voice here

Healing with Art : Intentional Self Creatives

Creative Self Expression : Creative Journaling to Narrate and Illustrate

Since the Creative Process IS the Intuitive Process, setting an intention to keep an illustrative art journal can become a way you practice Radical Self Care, without forcing it.

By intentionally writing and illustrating in a narrative journal, you are reconnecting with the Intuitive Body. You are not only healing but growing new brain connections and chemistries to appeal to your overall healthy well being.

Writing and Reflecting : not only is the art of writing a journal essential but it is the art of reflecting back and observing the thoughts and feelings from new perspectives that is transformational.

Mindful Practice Exercises : Expressive Art Journals :

1. <u>Radical Self Care Practice : Express your Self with Words and Images</u>
   <u>Mindful Journal</u> : Narrate and illustrate :
   - My art
   - My reflections
   - My observations
   - My insights

2. <u>Radical Self Care Intentional Practice</u> : DO NATURE
   <u>Mindful Journal</u> :
   - What did I do
   - Where did I go
   - How did I feel
   - What did I discover

3. <u>Radical Self Care Intentional Practice : DO MINDFUL MEDITATION</u>
   <u>Mindful Journal</u> :
   - What meditation practice did I choose?
   - What practice helps me focus on my breathing?
   - What practice helps quiet my thoughts?
   - What practice helps my body relax and release tension

4. <u>Radical Self Care Practice : Do SKY Breath Practices</u>
   <u>Mindful Journal</u> :
   - How did I feel before each practice?
   - how did I feel after each practice ?

5. <u>Radical Self Care Practice : Do Daily Yoga Prescriptives :</u>
   <u>Mindful Journal</u> :
   - Which practice did I do in the Morning?
   - Which practice did I do in the Evening?
   - What do I notice about how I feel different before and after my practice?

IN REFLECTION TO SUMMARIZE :

So you see, dear reader, you do NOT need to accept Burn Out as acceptable when you can practice Zen Centered Radical Self Care instead!

Zen Centered Radical Self Care both reverses the cycle of unhealthy Burn Out habits and heals the Intuitive Body's innate ability to restore rebalance and revitalize itself!

When you are ready to challenge Pain Body Beliefs like No Pain No Gain, you can reverse the cycle of feeling sick and tired and miserable pretending you are not!

BECOME CONSCIOUS

- Where does it hurt? When you see what hurts, you begin the Healing!

BECOME ACCOUNTABLE

- Treat your Intuitive Body with R-E-S-P-E-C-T
- AWAKEN to your Innate Ability to be a Miracle

BECOME AWARE

- What Zen Centered Radical Self Care options appeal to your need to heal Burnt Out?
- Practice – not per-fect – what you do to be more Present

BECOME INTENTIONAL

- Choose from a Place of Awareness
- How can you show your Body Reverence – or Respect- by the Radical Self Care plan you choose?

BE ENGAGED

~ Seize the moment NOW on behalf of Radical Self Care!

A CALL TO ACTION : WHAT IS YOURS?

Personal Narrative : *I knew I had turned the corner when I could envision something more for my self than helplessly immobilized in my mind and in my body. I could see my Self standing in calm strength, in clarity and light.*

Now that you can see….. Burn Out is NOT required, where will you choose to go from here?

So now dear reader, it is your turn to listen to your inner source of wisdom.

Vision : What does your Vision of "change possible" look like? What do you see?

In the End, do you know how you want to begin now to heal your Intuitive Body?

Exercise : Mindful Journal Prompts : use this space to make note of, observe and track your awareness steps.

Radical Self Care Exercises to Practice : Be Present Now :

1. Lessons Learned I Can Do Now:

2. Next step I can take Now :

3. How does it feel if I Vision this :

4. What is the Vision : draw write or take a picture of collage, vision board and put here.

5. What is my Next Step in the Now :

Here are some of my own examples to inspire you :

- Be patient and kind with your self
- Listen to your Intuitive Body for your "yes"
- Slow down.
- Pause and breathe slowly smoothly and deeply.
- Count to ten deep breaths.
- Tune in.
- Get Lost in Nature
- Do yoga daily
- Do art
- Write and draw in your journal
- Dance to music
- Anoint your body in essential oils
- Pet your pets
- Hug your Self and someone you love, linger long in the embrace
- Eat foods you love and foods that love your body
- Join a community of sisters who support you
- Light a scented candle
- Just say ommmmm

One last Mindful Inquiry :

How will you choose to honor and respect your Intuitive Body…..now that you have awakened to your own Zen Centered possibilities?

Printed in the United States
By Bookmasters